DIGITAL FISSURES

Studies in Critical Social Sciences Book Series

Haymarket Books is proud to be working with Brill Academic Publishers (www.brill.nl) to republish the *Studies in Critical Social Sciences* book series in paperback editions. This peer-reviewed book series offers insights into our current reality by exploring the content and consequences of power relationships under capitalism, and by considering the spaces of opposition and resistance to these changes that have been defining our new age. Our full catalog of *SCSS* volumes can be viewed at https://www.haymarketbooks .org/series_collections/4-studies-in-critical-social-sciences.

DIGITAL FISSURES

Bodies, Genders, Technologies

EDITED BY
CARLOTTA COSSUTTA, VALENTINA GRECO, ARIANNA MAINARDI AND STEFANIA VOLI

TRANSLATED BY
JULIA HEIM AND SOLE ANATRONE

Haymarket Books
Chicago, IL

First published in 2022 by Brill Academic Publishers, The Netherlands
© 2022 Koninklijke Brill NV, Leiden, The Netherlands

Published in paperback in 2023 by
Haymarket Books
P.O. Box 180165
Chicago, IL 60618
773-583-7884
www.haymarketbooks.org

ISBN: 979-8-88890-017-8

Distributed to the trade in the US through Consortium Book Sales and
Distribution (www.cbsd.com) and internationally through Ingram Publisher
Services International (www.ingramcontent.com).

This book was published with the generous support of Lannan Foundation,
Wallace Action Fund, and the Marguerite Casey Foundation.

Special discounts are available for bulk purchases by organizations and
institutions. Please call 773-583-7884 or email info@haymarketbooks.org for more
information.

Cover design by Jamie Kerry and Ragina Johnson.

Printed in the United States.

Library of Congress Cataloging-in-Publication data is available.

Contents

Figures

Notes on Contributors

Translator Biographies

Sole Anatrone
is an assistant professor of Italian studies at Vassar College, whose research focuses on questions of gender and sexuality, race, migration, and (post)colonialism. Her publications include: "Almeno non hai un nome da negra:" Race, Gender and National Belonging in Laila Wadia's Amiche per la pelle. *Gender/Sexuality/Italy Journal*; and "Disciplining Narratives and Damaged Identities in Rossana Campo's Lezioni di arabo," *California Italian Studies*. She is also co-editor and contributor to *Queering Italian Media* (Lexington Books, 2020). She is a co-founder of Asterisk, a taskforce that offers workshops to university faculty, students, and staff geared toward fostering LGBTQIA+ inclusivity inside and outside the classroom.

Julia Heim
is a lecturer of Italian studies at the University of Pennsylvania and a translator of queer theory, art criticism, and the children's book series Geronimo Stilton. Heim holds a PhD in Comparative Literature from the CUNY Graduate Center. She is a cofounder of Asterisk, a higher education LGBTQIA+ inclusivity task force, and her research focuses on LGBTQIA+ representation in contemporary Italian television. Her most recent publications are the co-edited volume *Queering Italian Media*, (Lexington Press, 2020) and "Italian LGBTQ Representation in Transnational Television" in *The Journal of Italian Cinema & Media Studies* which came out in February 2020.

Cover Artist Biography

Carla Gannis
is a transmedia artist based in Brooklyn, New York. She produces works that consider the uncanny complications between grounded and virtual reality, nature and artifice, science and science fiction in contemporary culture. Fascinated by digital semiotics, Gannis takes a horror vacui approach to her artistic practice, culling inspiration from networked communication, art and feminist histories, emerging technologies and speculative design.

Author Biographies

Angela Balzano

is a precarious Foucauldian and feminist researcher, convinced that in the interstice between social, biological, and technological reproduction there lie many knots that must be undone. She has translated the works of Rosi Braidotti (*Il postumano,* 2014; *Itinerari etici. Per una politica affermativa, 2017*) and Cooper and Waldby (*Biolavoro globale. Corpi e nuova mandopera,* 2015). Her research and activism revolve around sexuality and reproductive rights (and the lack thereof): contraception, voluntary termination of pregnancy, artificial insemination and surrogate pregnancies. After getting her philosophy degree she completed her doctorate in Law and New Technologies at the University of Bologna, where she is now a Temporary Research Fellow.

Rachele Borghi

is a geographer, a professor at the Sorbonne in Paris, an academic porno-activist, and, with Slavina, she is a member of the collective Zarra Bonheur. Her work focuses on the deconstruction of dominant norms that materialize in specific places, and contaminate certain spaces. Her research is based on feminist and decolonial epistemology through which she tries to rupture the walls of the university, and disseminate knowledge, ideas and practices. Her core interest is in the body as a space, as an instrument of resistance, and as a vehicle for relationships. She is a huge fan of Monique Wittig and bell hooks, and she believes that you can be born or you can become a guerrilla fighter (www.zarrabonheur.org – https://cv.archives-ouvertes.fr/rachele-borghi).

Carlotta Cossutta, Valentina Greco, Arianna Mainardi and Stefania Voli

are transfeminist precarious researchers in various disciplines, they study bodies, sexualities, and technologies. They enter and exit the narrow margins of academia, mixing theory and political practice. They live between Milan and Bologna–but most often on trains–bridging the physical distances through digital platforms.

eva kunin

was born in 2011 as a queer digital identity experiment with the intention of exploring the potential of web 2.0 in transmitting and spreading cultural ideas and projects in open content formats. the literary inspiration at the time of its birth was found in John Fante's "bankrupt" characters; she is one of them. a libertine. organizer of disciplinary intrusions. fleeing from categories and vertical hierarchies (even in her orthography). of a senseless and totally unjustified optimism: she believes [powerfully] in the power of creative acts. even the smallest ones. because she knows that the world. though it insists on hiding it from us every day. is full of open hearts. attentive gazes. curious and wise minds. capable of seizing them. madly in love with the city of Lisbon ... she believes she has already died there * (https://facebook.com/photo.php?fbid=255439147909769&set=pb.100003310585917.-2207520000.1522736793.&type=3&theater).

Diego Marchante "Genderhacker"

(http://genderhacker.net) is a transfeminist activist and transmedia artist. A doctor of Fine Arts from the University of Barcelona, "Genderhacker" has worked as an instructor of fine arts at the same university since 2008. In 2016 they finished their doctoral thesis *Transbutch, Luchas fronterizas de género entre el arte y la política,* an archive of social movements and artistic practices that deal with questions of gender in the Spanish context from a queer and transfeminist perspective (http://archivo-t.net).

Obiezione Respinta

(*Objection Denied*) are a group of students, many of whom are off campus, and are precarious laborers who, for several years now, have worked to investigate the state of health services both in Pisa and nationally, in particular those services tied to the voluntary termination of pregnancy and contraception. Since March 8, 2017 we have managed the site obiezionerespinta.info, which hosts an interactive map where you can mark the presence of conscientious objectors in pharmacies, hospitals and medical facilities. Currently, in addition to the map, we run a legal help desk and a gynecological help desk in Limonaia – Zona Rosa to supplement the lacking services in our city.

Lucía Egaña Rojas

(http://lucysombra.org) is a graduate in Fine Arts and Documentary Studies, and has a doctorate in Audiovisual Communications. Currently Lucía has a Hangar Artist Residency, and is part of the academic board of MACBA's (Barcelona Contemporary Art Museum) Program for Independent Studies. Lucía writes and researches transfeminism, pornography, free software and errors. Recently, Lucía published the book *Atrincheradas en la cane. Lecturas en torno a las prácticas postpornográficas.*

Elisa Virgili

has a doctorate of philosophy in Social Sciences. Elisa works on gender studies and queer theories, and in particular on the relationship between gender and language. She trains as a boxer in a public gym where she tries to understand the relationship between gender and sport. Lately, she has discovered accelerationist theories and, for the first time, here she has tried to grapple with them.

Ludovico (Vick) Virtù

is a precarious migrant researcher and transfeminist activist who is currently graduating from Radboud University Nijmegen in Holland. Sicilian in origin, Vick is still not sure where to call "home." He has lived between Bologna, London, Beijing, Barcelona and Utrecht. Vick co-organizes seminars and events on the depathologization of trans transitions, the dynamics of exclusion/inclusion within academia, and alternative representations of gender and sexuality in cultural production. He is the co-editor of the special volume *Trans Materialities* for the journal "GJSS – Graduate Journal of Social Science" (forthcoming), and he collaborates with the Movimento identità tans (MIT) in Bologna.

Translators' Note

Digital Fissures is a work of plurality. It is a collection of transfeminist writings testifying to the challenges we are confronted with as queer-bodied, queer-minded thinkers, as well as to the challenges posed by these transfeminist scholars and activists to the systems of power that seek to marginalize, oppress and disenfranchise. In this volume we hear stories of academic activists in Paris, queer cartographers in Rome, and (trans)gender archivists in Barcelona, among many others advocating for a reimagining of the interaction between our bodies and the power systems that organize our world. By adding to the mix our voices as translators, and our own multiply-situated identities, we participate in this call to action, amplifying these stories and making them accessible to a global, English-speaking audience. It is with this spirit of collaboration that we invite you, the reader, to be an active partner as you bring your own experiences to these pages.

One of the consistent themes throughout the pages of this volume is precisely this commitment to bringing the personal to bear on the political, on the radical, on the bodily, on the technological. We see this for example when Rachele Borghi takes us on stage with her as her collaborative ethnography-performance challenges the norms of academia at Paris's Sorbonne University. Similarly, the queer creator of *eva kunin* invites us into the intimacy of their Roman hangouts, bars and bookstores as they reimagine cartography, urban space and the line between the physical ('real world') and the digital ('virtual world'). And in "Dis/organizing DIY Sexuality: A Trans Perspective," Ludovico Virtù weaves together a discussion of the intimate pleasures of sex toys with a critique of consumerism and capitalist production. In each case, the divide between author and subject is intentionally blurred to force us to pay attention to our own practices of distancing and interpretation.

This translation is our participation in this praxis, in the creation of language and ideas through our bodies and technologies. We see this work as a mediated interpretation of the Italian text, which is then mediated by you, the reader, who positions it and understands it within the context of your own lived experience. To use translator Kate Briggs's metaphor, "When the gym is so full of bodies I can't see the instructor, I copy the woman in front of me, and the woman behind me copies me in turn. In this way we share the moves around. We get to dance them–the pleasure of actually getting to dance them! Someone else's moves, only this time made with my own body–falling in and out of sync with each other, with the music, with hip hop, tango, ballet."[1] This is how we understand our collaborative translation: we learn from one another, speaking the same thing differently, together, touched and affected by one another's participation in the conversation of our collective words. We are working together with you to produce new meaning that is active and transformative. In this way, as translators and readers, we are participating in the transtechnofeminism that is figured and refigured throughout these pages.

Briggs' metaphor brings to light this sense of action or movement that is so present in the act of translation; one might think that this is a direct movement between two languages, a game of substitution from one Italian term to the corresponding English one, but in truth it is much messier. In fact, our interest in this process is in its movement, movement that involves our bodies and the generative bodies of our work together, just like the bodies at the gym teaching each other through a sweaty game of bodily telephone. The very act of our play and our choices moves and shifts the languages in and through which we work, dismantling notions of linguistic stability. In "A Scene of Intimate Entanglements, or, Reckoning with the 'Fuck' of Translation," Elena Basile explains that languages and subjectivities are constantly policed in an effort to maintain the fiction of their boundaries, but "the movement of translation, when attentively pursued as movement, puts pressure on the very frame of linguistic enclosure upon which the purported representational stability of source and target texts is predicated."[2] So what we have with translation is a performance of destabilization. The entanglements of languages and of words is a performance of unraveling, of coming undone.

This unraveling is at the heart of this very text. In the original title *Smagliature digitali*, the word '*Smagliature*'–in Italian–speaks to a process of unraveling and the word, like the action, is elusive, taking us in various directions at the same time as it unfurls towards different meanings and contexts. As we approached the task of translating the title, we followed these different threads, pulling on each one as we unraveled the piece and built it anew, testing English terms for their fit with the meaning, the substance and feel of the body we were remaking and the game we were playing.

Smagliature is a very embodied, very physical word; the unraveling it evokes can be textile, like the runs in tights, or organic, like stretchmarks on the body, two notions that are often associated with women through the garments of

---

1   Kate Briggs, *This Little Art* (London: Fitzcarraldo Editions, 2017), 212.
2   Elena Basile, "A Scene of Intimate Entanglements, or, Reckoning with the 'Fuck' of Translation," in *Queering Translation, Translating the Queer*, eds. Brian James Baer, Klaus Kaindl (Routledge: New York, 2017), 31, 30.

femininity and the travails of childbirth. Anna Gorchakovskaya chose this thread in translating the title as *Digital Stretch Marks* for her review of the Italian edition,[3] thus centering the female body and nodding to the ways the text sheds light on and dismantles gender expectations. We felt pulled in a slightly different direction, however, as our attention and affect were caught (snagged?) by something that emerged as we read and translated the editors' introduction: "society changes only if the relations of subordination change, and this must start with oppressed and excluded subjectivities, it must start with the margins, from the sweaters off their backs: from the fissures."[4] Here they call for change to begin from the sweaters off the backs of the oppressed, nodding—for us, as American-trained feminist reader-translators—to the backs, the bodies, the 'theory in the flesh,' of those whose intersectionalities and feminisms we read and teach in *This Bridge Called My Back*. As Cherríe Moraga writes in the intro that foundational feminist text:

> I watch the divide between generations widen with time and technology. I watch how desperately we need political memory, so that we are not always imagining ourselves the ever-inventors of our revolution; so that we are humbled by the valiant efforts of our foremothers; and so, with humility and a firm foothold in history, we can enter upon an informed and re-envisioned strategy for social/political change in the decades ahead.[5]

We foreground this reference to the backs and bodies of *This Bridge* as it speaks to a genealogy of disruption and continuation that is marked on the collective and the individual body. The technological changes Moraga writes about are revisited, mapped out and explored anew in the pages of this new text, as are the ways they can be used to preserve the legacies of queer and feminist actions that came before. This connection between these two bodies of work, and the bodies of which they speak, is reinforced by the word itself, *smagliature*, which, when broken down presents us with *maglia* or 'sweater,' and that negating 's' before it, which in Italian is often used to signify the word's direct opposite [as in the example formato/sformato = formed/deformed]. Thus, *smaglia*

3 Anna Gorchakovskaya, "Digital Stretch Marks: Bodies, Genders and Technologies," *Digicult*, Accessed July 18th, 2019. http://digicult.it/books/digital-stretch-marks-bodies-genders-and -technologies/.

4 Cossutta et al, "Where the Margins Aren't Borders," infra, 20.

5 Cherríe Moraga, "Catching Fire: Preface to the Fourth Edition," in *This Bridge Called My Back: Writings by Radical Women of Color*, eds. Cherríe Moraga and Gloria Anzaldúa (Albany: SUNY Press, 2015), XIX.

could signify being without a *maglia,* losing the sweaters from our backs. In the case of this text, *smagliature* is modified by the term 'digital,' so that the digital is an integral part of the fabric and the tear; to change this grammatical dynamic would misrepresent the ways that the digital is woven through the bodies, technologies, and genders explored by the book. We imagine a sort of bodily 'glitch,'[6] but felt compelled to keep some trace of the affective, physical memory that inheres in notions of scars from growth or childbirth, and the trauma and cold of having sweaters torn off our back. In this way we found ourselves playing with the fissure, looking at a stretch mark that had opened to a wound, an unraveling that was rupturing the cybersphere. Linguistically and figuratively then, fissure extends to the socio-politics within the intersections of bodies, genders, and politics. We wanted to mark the difficulty of the English translation–perhaps even playfully–by choosing a word that neither of us completely pronounces with confidence (fizz-ure? fiss-you-err? fisher?). Just as Briggs learns the modified, transformed dance moves from the bodies around her, so too is the translator's dance made up precisely of moves created by slippages between and through both working languages.

Philosopher Lauren Berlant notes: "Objects are always looser than they appear. Objectness is only a semblance, a seeming, a projection effect of interest in a thing we are trying to stabilize."[7] There are deep parallels here between the claims we are making about the play of translation that occurs because of linguistic instability–despite common notions that would have one believe in the concreteness of the sign-referent bond–and Berlant's understanding of the instability of objectness, an objectness upon which our infrastructures depend. This parallel highlights the ways in which the politics and activism of the chapters in this book are in direct conversation with our work as translators, as we all point to the tenuousness of the social groundwork on which we tread. As readers will see, technological apparatuses and digital spaces have shaped much more than the micro-publics that constitute our affective communities. We share a common digisphere with the writers whose words we translate, a 'commons' whose better power, for Berlant, "is to point to a way to view what's broken in sociality, the difficulty of convening a world conjointly, although it is inconvenient and hard, and to offer incitements to imagining

---

6   With this elaboration of "glitch" we are explicitly referencing Lauren Berlant's use of "glitch" in her elaboration of the relationship between the commons and infrastructure in "The Commons: Infrastructures for Troubling Times" in *Environment and Planning D: Society and Space* 34(3), 2016, pp. 393–419.

7   Lauren Berlant, "The Commons: Infrastructures for Troubling Times," *Environment and Planning D: Society and Space*, vol. 34: 3: 394.

a livable provisional life."[8] One of the strengths of the digital commons, as Genderhacker proves in their chapter "Transcyborgdyke: A Transfeminist and Queer Perspective on Hacking the Archive," is that it makes visible and accessible an archive of the work and legacies of previous publics. It helps us live within a commons that is not bound by time, and this, in turn, gives us not only perspective, but frameworks. The legacies that the queers and feminists that preceded us provide are building blocks; we do not start from nothing.

In this way, if we go back to the notion of the glitch for a moment, a glitch within the space of the digital might provide us an occasion to collectively reflect on and reshape those infrastructures that give shape to our lives, a glitch that marks a moment where tools like technology might be taken up. From the place of this glitch, this fissure, new commons, new intimate publics— who affectively come together and reject the 'brokenness' of this glitch—are formed.

Together with you, reader, we seek to shake the building blocks of the infrastructures that establish and preserve racist heteronormative misogynist institutions and ways of living.

Julia Heim and Sole Anatrone

---

8   Berlant, 395.

A Note on the English Edition

A translation is the invention of a new book. The last inseparable layer of sediment from the original text, and yet distinctly different.

Digital Fissures, like any other book, wasn't born the moment it was published, but rather, a good year before. Before becoming paper it was synapses, pixels, notes, trips, seminars, conferences, meetings, websites.

Now we are reading it in a language other than the one in which it was written and we are the first to rediscover it. Thanks to the power and depth of the authors who wrote the essays within it, we learn that *Digital Fissures* is a book that speaks to the present even though it was written in the recent past.

A translation is not just a transposition or a mimetic exercise; it is an attempt to contaminate worlds.

Here, translation is a way of trespassing, pushing our southern European transfeminist perspectives beyond their borders. Trespassing is part of our geography of margins. Speaking of margins, we want to remember bell hooks in this current moment from which we speak. bell hooks is in *Digital Fissures* more than was made explicit in the Italian edition, and we want to take advantage of the English version to thank her.

The fissure is an unmendable tear. From our transfeminist perspective it contains the marginal and the vulnerable. While cisheteropatriarchal society demands two bodies and assigns two roles, the fissure undoes the binarism and, in the transparency of thinning skin, reveals the norms' other.

The fissure is the transgression (hooks), the monstrosity (Stryker), the art of failure (Halberstam), opposition to enforced identity (Aizura).

Digital Fissures was born as an act of contamination, an interweaving, a translation of debates, of stories and practices that spoke to the relationship between bodies, genders and technologies; it began with the specificity of our being situated within Italy, in a yesterday very close to today. *Digital Fissures* was a textual iteration of the story and the genealogy of an Italian transfeminism formed in the marginal spaces of cities and politics, in the cooperatives and the creative battle against a rhetoric-laden catholic, patriarchal social structure. In its encounter with technologies, this battle is capable of generating worlds like FikaFutura or MeduseCyborg, among others, (these are, not by chance, part of the same story as AgenziaX, the publishing house for the Italian edition); capable of generating experiences that mix care with hacking, vibrators with pamphlets. A battle that was frequently fueled by resources from other parts of southern Europe, resources that spoke more Castilian, Catalan or Basque than English, resources that created networks that were often invisible to official genealogies. It is a battle that crosses into the present. *Digital Fissures* tried, in this way, to fill a void as it drew on the legacy of a multifaceted and fractured whole, without piecing it back together.

Bringing this journey into another language doesn't just mean translating these texts, it means giving space to thoughts that are born in another language, thoughts that incorporate terms–often English ones–from technology and debates on gender, dirtying them with the many dialects that speak them. The process of translation covered a span of time that invested our bodies, the modes and practices of our beings that we had described in the introduction to the Italian edition as being marked by an im/materiality devoid of hierarchy. In this interval–between the publication of the Italian edition and the English one–we learned that a global pandemic imposes hierarchies between digital and analog spaces, times, desires, bodies and technologies. Social distancing and the economic recession redefined the marginal spaces, spaces that became more and more crowded. The subjects that live in these spaces today are the same as they were before, but now they are more: domestic violence and femicide increased during the lockdown, and this ascending curve seems to have inserted itself perfectly in the context of a structural health emergency; the worst consequences in terms of livability and privation are those that hit poor-migrant people and people asking for asylum, LGBTQIA+, sex-workers, HIV-positive folk, cis women involved in abusive relationships, and people without stable housing.

Technologies have a strange relationship to time. Often associated with novelty, with acceleration, with productivity, they participate in the construction of a precarious, exclusionary present. But they are also tools that we construct from the ground up, tools we appropriate to produce an alternate pace of life, to build memories and ecologies of cyberfeminist relations. In the context created by the pandemic, our bodies and our feelings continue to give life to practices of care, to relationships, to sexuality, and to participation, including in spaces mediated by technology. From our positionality we like to think that the effect of time on (technological?) fissures is unforeseen and does not respond to a prescribed linearity.

In keeping with the transformative potential of transfeminism that emerged from *Digital Fissures*, we rediscover a new potential in the assemblage of practices, experiences and embodiments of these translated words and terms with which this project speaks four years later.

Carlotta Cossutta, Valentina Greco, Arianna Mainardi and Stefania Voli
January 16th, 2022

CHAPTER 1

Where the Margins Aren't Borders

Carlotta Cossutta, Valentina Greco, Arianna Mainardi and Stefania Voli

I wasn't planning on giving an account of myself, but rather, on breaking completely.

ELEONORA DANCO

• • •

Woman's body is science fiction.

FRANCESCA GENTI

• • •

You are as constructed as me; the same anarchic Womb has birthed us both. I call upon you to investigate your nature as I have been compelled to confront mine. I challenge you to risk abjection and flourish as well as have I. Heed my words, and you may well discover the seams and sutures in yourself.

SUSAN STRYKER

• •
•

This book wouldn't exist without digital technologies.

We, the four editors, live in different places; we work in places that are different from the ones in which we live; we were born in different places than the ones in which we live and work. Our transfeminist activism brings us together often, but in those moments there is no time for anything else.

This book comes from our "virtual meetings" on Skype, WhatsApp, Google Drive, and from our email correspondence. The people who wrote the contributions that make up this volume live in Italy, Holland, France, Spain, Finland, and England, and are often in places other than their places of birth. We contacted them because we know them personally, because we have read and loved them, meeting them at a conference, or thanks to private messages, chats on social networks, or finding their emails from websites or blogs.

The tables on which we work are divided "by thousands of physical kilometers, held together by the prosthetic support of the internet [...] the Newtonian categories of space and time (topology and chronology) seem to collapse. We float. We look at each other and I ask myself where this gaze is located, how is it possible to look at one another when what the eyes see are not other eyes but just the image of eyes on a screen."[1]

This book is a transfeminist queer cyborg.

There is no hierarchy between the spaces that united us; we occupied them from time to time so we could be together.

There is no hierarchy of bodies; our fingers always touched as we typed on the computer keyboard.

"The boundary between physical and non-physical is very imprecise for us,"[2] there is no hierarchy, there is complexity.

This book is a transfeminist queer cyborg that looks through a kaleidoscope.

The pieces that make it up are multifaceted, they are in dialogue with one another, they agree, they conflict, they provoke, and they respond to one another, like self-contained episodes in a series with a common thread.

The reflections on the relationship between bodies/technologies/cyberspace often focus on the processes of disembodiment, de-materialization, with enthusiastic tones on the one hand, and with catastrophic ones on the other, "they oscillate between the delirium of omnipotence and the paranoia of total impotence;"[3] but "looking critically at the contradictions of technology, as well as the current relationships of power, doesn't necessarily coincide with a condemnation of technology."[4] They are polarized positions that willingly tend to cancel out everything in between. Concrete vs. Abstract, Physical vs. Virtual, Space vs. Cyberspace, they are all two-sided coins, they are proof of how difficult it is to break free from constraint and to think differently.

---

1   Paul B. Preciado, "La tecnologia cambia i corpi e le coscienze," *Internazionale*, 30 January 2017. (https://www.internazionale.it/opinione/paul-preciado/2017/01/30/tecnologia-corpi -coscienze).

2   Donna Haraway, *Simians, Cyborgs and Women: The Reinvention of Nature*, (New York: Routledge, 1991), 152.

3   Paul B. Preciado, "La tecnologia cambia i corpi e le coscienze."

4   Brunella Casalini, Federico Zappino, "Preface," in Karin Harrasser, *Corpi 2.0. Sulla dilatabilità tecnica dell'Uomo*, (goWare: Florence 2018).

FIGURE 1.1   Binarism is for computer, "Non una di meno global protest," March 8th 2018
PHOTO BY MICHELE LAPINI, GRACIOUSLY PROVIDED THE PHOTOGRAPHER

"Binarism is for computer," read a fuchsia-colored sign with black writing at a Non una di meno protest in Bologna, on March 8th, 2018.[5] But binary thinking is soothing, it gives the impression of making a choice, it's like an "all inclusive" option, it makes you feel proper and, maybe even more importantly, it makes you feel supported.

This book is a transfeminist queer cyborg that refuses to play heads or tails.

If "in the dominant culture the default operating system is Windows," the default sexuality is "white, monogamous, singleparent; habit is a niche market," writes Lucía Egaña Rojas; only cognitive instruments that can help us recognize and challenge the implicit hierarchies and systems of power in a polarized and dichotomized system of thought can lead us toward "a transfeminist technology [that] is based on the unrepeatability of each small gesture, on serendipity and on chance."[6] Questioning the categories and tools through

---

5   *Non una di meno* is a trans/feminist movement with chapters all over Italy dedicated to fighting gender and sexual oppression and discrimination. Following the lead of the Argentinian group *Ni una menos,* the Italian version initially took form in 2016 in response to the high number of femicides and misogynist media and juridical responses to those violences. For more information see: https://nonunadimeno.wordpress.com/.

6   Lucía Egaña Rojas, "Technofeminism," infra, 28.

which we observe the world in order to understand the new relationships between bodies, genders, and technologies, opens up a series of epistemological questions about the redefinition of the relationship between knowledge and technology. In this way, Donna Haraway[7] contests the concept of objectivity, insisting on the need to recognize each point of view as partial. Feminist thought on the construction of knowledge lays claim, in fact, to a self-conscious practice in which "personal stories" are used as tools to illuminate theoretical choices, where differences are considered relational and not intrinsic perspectives, where bodies are recognized as having a social and cultural awareness. From where, therefore, do the authors of this book speak? The authors of this book develop a knowledge around, and with, technologies that feed, first and foremost, off bodies and experiences; this is an embodied knowledge because it begins from the central concept of feminist epistemology that understands the subject as situated in a specific context. In this way, a process of knowledge construction is born that is embodied and in movement, and that redefines the boundaries between the margins and the center, challenging reassuring dichotomies of thought and practice.

Technologies can be used to support processes of open and shared knowledge construction, putting emphasis on the collective aspect of knowledge. As the contributions of eva kunin and Obiezione Respinta (Objection Denied) show, these become spaces of participation and sharing that come in the form, for example, of an interactive map where "[t]he physical and virtual plans of vindication coexist and weave together starting with the collective experience we lived through the mobilizing acts of Non una di meno."[8] Thus, new forms of political participation are opened up that join the individual and collective dimensions, the lived spaces on and offline, creating a web of relations that feeds off bodies, situated knowledges, and technologies.

Reflecting on knowledge is crucial for calling into question the very "nature" of technologies, and for recognizing their social and relational character, so as to dissolve it. The unifying link between the essays in this book is the awareness of this reciprocity, focusing on the relations of power that are at times challenged, and at times reproduced, both within and with technologies; technologies are a theme both as a source and as a consequence of the structuring of the relations of power that are defined on the basis of gender. From the microwave, to the telephone, to the birth control pill, to robotics and software, technology plays a part in the structure of our social roles, and the

---

7 Donna Haraway, "Situated Knowledges: The Science Question in Feminism and the Privilege of Partial Perspective," *Feminist Studies* 14.3, (1998), 575–99.

8 Obiezione Respinta, "Objection Denied," infra, 56.

marginalization of subjectivities that do not conform to the cis-hetero-white norm on the part of the technological community, norms that have a profound influence on the content, the design, the technology, and the use of technological artefacts.[9] One of the threads that brings together feminist scholars working in this field is the way they have approached, deconstructed and elaborated on the exclusion of some subjectivities with respect to others in the technological world (in social structures, individual and collective identities, and symbolic representations). The feminist perspective on the social study of technologies has paid particular attention not just to the power of social institutions in giving shape to technology, but also to the power of subjects to appropriate it. The meaning of technological artifacts is built through a process of negotiation between agents; there is no unifying meaning or usage established in the moment of their ideation; to the contrary, they are open to varying interpretations, and based on these interpretations subjectivities intervene, negotiating their meaning and redefining it.

Technologies are a contentious object, met with tensions and ambivalences, in which we find the space for political processes of subjectification.

The digital is spatial, Janet H. Murray affirms in 1997,[10] individuating spatiality as one of the primary characteristics of digital media. If it is true that, in general, "most of our fundamental concepts are organized in terms of one or more spatialization metaphors,"[11] it is even more true for the internet and for digital technologies; the numerous spatial metaphors that we use to describe our experiences on the web are proof: digital *environment, navigate* online, *surf* the web, *enter* a site, virtual *town hall,* or information *highway.*

"Free streets are made by the women who cross them" isn't a slogan, it is a project, a thought that comes to life, and it is true for electronic streets as well. The statement: "the spaces, including cyber ones, create the non-normative subjectivities that cross them," implies recognizing that even spaces aren't unambiguous, they transform, and above all, they can be transformed.

From a transfeminist point of view, the body itself becomes a space, "[t]he body is a space where performance comes alive and has worth as a tool of resistance and rupture of the norms that regulate public spaces. From this

9   Judy Wacjmac, "From Women and Technology to Gendered Technoscience Information," *Community and Society* 10(3), 2007, 287–298.

10   Janet H. Murray, *Hamlet on the Holodeck: The Future of Narrative in Cyberspace,* (New York: Simon and Schuster, 1997).

11   George Lakoff and Mark Johnson, *Metaphors We Live By,* (Chicago: University of Chicago Press, 1980), 17.

FIGURE 1.2   Street art, rue de Francs Bourgeois, Paris
            PHOTO BY VALENTINA GRECO

perspective the body can become a tool for the transgression of dominant social norms in a determined space."[12]

The body is the biopolitical space par excellance, it is the space that defines spaces; the violence of the norm acts on it, change acts through it.

The body (re)creates the space it crosses, changing its features. To misquote *Alice in Wonderland*: "If you knew him like I know him, you wouldn't speak of HIM. You'd speak of THEM."[13]

---

12   Rachele Borghi, "Notes From the Center's Margins," infra, 90.

13   "'If you knew Time as well as I do,' said the Hatter, 'you wouldn't talk about wasting *it*. It's *him*.'" [Lewis Carroll, *The Adventures of Alice in Wonderland*].

Space, like feminism, like body, is multiple, even when you read it in the singular. We think of the body-space in terms of a somatech (Preciado), or, rather, as an archive of living political fictions that in no way constitute a single corpus. Digital technologies today occupy a surface that is much larger than this archive, because of the unavoidable (since they are desired but also endured) ties that our bodies have weaved with them.

"In reality, this archive is a body, or rather, this archive is my body. [...] This body-archive of mine did not appear from nothing, its existence would have been impossible without the recognition of the genealogy of other gender and sexual dissidents."[14]

However, this space-archive undergoes continual transformations and "If 'cyberspace' once offered the promise of escaping the strictures of essentialist identity categories, the climate of contemporary social media has swung forcefully in the other direction, and has become a theatre where these prostrations to identity are performed."[15]

Technology is always the product of a social organization that uses it to reproduce relations of power and categorizations, and the gesture of deconstructing it is a political gesture in itself because it breaks the chains of reproduction, inserting variations, awareness, positionality, and materiality.

Refusing to use the master's tools, therefore, doesn't mean renouncing technology, but rather giving up the organization from which it is produced and recreated. Therefore, it is fundamental to take into account Rachele Borghi and Zarra Bonheur's invitation to turn your gaze toward the margins rather than the center, toward the inappropriate uses of technology rather than its linear development, because this "allows us not only to see the margins, but above all to see that they are inhabited, that for every center-space there is a corresponding occupied margin, freed spaces that can become the ground on which to build utopia."[16]

In the various contributions to this book, the margins and the borders are effectively investigated from a variety of different aspects: from those between the body and technologies, to very concrete urban spaces (like, for eva kunin, the experience of an ebook that becomes a stroll).

Reflecting on the border brings to light how technologies are used more and more for defending personal and collective security. And this desire to safeguard breaks another border, between the private and the public, between the

---

14   Diego Marchante "Genderhacker," "Transcyborgdyke," infra, 100.

15   Laboria Cuboniks, "Xenofeminism," *Xenofeminist Manifesto*, 2018, https://laboriacubon iks.net/manifesto/xenofeminism-a-politics-for-alienation/.

16   Rachele Borghi, "Notes from the Center's Margins," infra, 97.

intimate and the visible. This breaking down of borders produces a rupture that reveals the pervasiveness of security tech devices within homes and in public spaces, where all opaque, unseen, dark corners must be eliminated. In this sense there is a resemblance between the body, which has been examined by medical technologies, parceled to the genome, and public or private spaces under constant surveillance. These are the same mobile apparatuses that we use daily to bring the outside world into our private spaces (through news, work, contacts, etc.), and intimacy into the public space (photos, messages, heart monitors, etc.). However, this shifting of borders not only increases our risk of constant surveillance, as it does with the body, it also pushes us to reproduce social and gender norms in whatever spaces we occupy, because every space can be immediately social.

Even in this case, therefore, in order to subvert we must first dissolve the categories we feel secure with, and recognize a complexity that exceeds hierarchies, and we must destroy a social order. As Laboria Cuboniks stresses, we must rethink the lines between inclusion and exclusion, and between public and private spaces, redefining the terms under investigation: "Let us set sights on augmented homes of shared laboratories, of communal media and technical facilities. [...] If we want to break the inertia that has kept the moribund figure of the nuclear family unit in place, which has stubbornly worked to isolate women from the public sphere, and men from the lives of their children, while penalizing those who stray from it, we must overhaul the material infrastructure and break the economic cycles that lock it in place."[17] In acting against the surveillance and privatization supported by security technologies we must open and share, even technological tools, to avoid reproducing the hierarchies that continue to tow the lines of gender and racialization. But, we must also reclaim the importance of opaque, non-visible, unseen spaces, because, as Charlotte Perkins Gilman maintained at the beginning of the 20th century, "the more broadly socialised we become, the more we need our homes to rest in. [...] Private, secluded, sweet, wholly our own; not invaded by any trade or work or business, not open to the crowd,"[18] and, we might add, not open to a surveillance that is too normalized.

Much has changed since the years in which the first feminist experiments on the web took shape. The new digital spaces and the mass spread of mobile technologies change the relationship with anonymity, corporeality, and creativity. As we've said, life on the internet is scarcely decontextualized or disembodied;

---

17   Laboria Cuboniks, "Xenofeminism."
18   Charlotte Perkins Gilman, *The Home: Its Work and Influence,* (New York: McClure, Phillips, & Co., 1903), 347.

at the same time virtual experiences, or rather, online experiences, penetrate daily reality, becoming indistinguishable from it. What follows is that online activity is strongly influenced by the politics of offline spaces, both materially and symbolically. According to Kember and Zylinska[19] we must think of the media not just as simple use-objects, but rather we must recognize our almost symbiotic relationship with the media both socio-culturally and biologically; digital technologies enter our lives and mediate identity and relationships daily.

The internet is an ambivalent relational space, it appears to be a tool for experimenting with identity and relationships, and at the same time a locus of control and normalization. The possibility of expressing one's identity through these media depends on many factors, first and foremost the specific technological allowances that permit or inhibit different types of self-representation and interaction. If, on the one hand, our digital practices partake in processes of normalization that inhibit forms of experimentation, on the other, our actions with and through digital media work to force them to do so.

Studies that interrogate the web as an apparatus of gender control and surveillance suggest that its real transformative possibility—which comes from the relationship with digital environments—depends on the capacity of subjects to control their own information. Furthermore, the most recent cyberfeminist studies[20] emphasize the need to look at how the relationship between new media and neoliberalism is stronger and stronger, and the borders between self-determination/subjectivity/agency and processes of market-led identity construction become more and more muddled.[21] With the intention of updating cyberfeminist critical thought, given the changing social and technological landscape, Gajjala and Ju Oh note that for cyberfeminists there are new challenges and new questions: how do we face those attractive discourses that describe the internet as a space of personal and collective realization, when we suspect that digital technologies are intrinsically tied to the logic of neoliberalism?[22]

The answer these scholars give is to look at different types of online participation, but to be careful not to believe that all marginalized voices lie outside systems of oppression, and not to believe that yours is a privileged

---

19 Sara Kember and Joanna Zylinska, *Life After New Media: Mediation as a Vital Process* (Boston: MIT Press, 2012).

20 A very recent work on this topic is: Daniele Gambetta, ed. *Datacrazia. Politica, cultura algoritmica e conflitti al tempo dei big data (Datacracy. Politics, Algorithmic Culture and Conflict in the Age of Big Data)* (Ladispoli: D. Editore, 2018).

21 Radhika Gajjala and Yeon Ju Oh, *Cyberfeminism 2.0*, (New York: Peter Lang Publishing, 2012).

22 Ibid.

FIGURE 1.3   "Hello is it me you're looking for?" Street art,
             Teufelsberg, Berlin
             PHOTO BY STEFANIA VOLI

interpretation simply because you consider yourself more epistemologically competent at identifying political and social structures. Instead of looking at the internet as an indisputable space of freedom, they suggest looking at its ambivalence. In other words, bringing to light how the relationships of power at the base of gender are simultaneously reinforced, called into question, and deconstructed with and through digital technologies.

We must, as we've said, deconstruct the dichotomies that seem to have remained implicit, and focus on technologies created for and by new alliances. Intersectional studies,[23] are among some of the disciplines that can offer tools for dismantling a discourse on technologies rooted in a geography-based privilege that has governed the majority of analyses in this area.

---

23   Koen Leurs, "Performing Gender and Ethnicity in Socio-Technological Networks: Entangling Feminist Technoscience and Postcolonial Studies," *International Journal of Feminist Technoscience,* 2009.

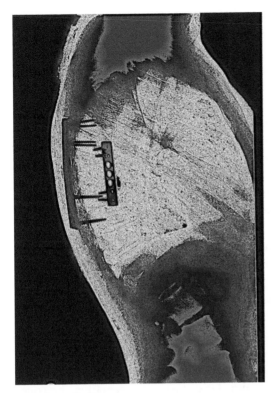

FIGURE 1.4   D7 D8
PHOTO BY STEFANIA VOLI, PHOTOSHOP
BY VALENTINA GRECO

In 1994, Susan Stryker wrote an article we can now consider a political trans manifesto in which she evokes Mary Shelley's fantasy horror story
Frankenstein.[24] Inspired by the scene in which the monster, turning to his creator for the first time, reveals himself to be something different and "more than"
what he had imagined, the trans historian and activist argues that dominant
medical knowledge associates transgender subjectivity with Frankenstein's
monstrosity. In this metaphor, the trans body is a place that lies outside the
natural order and, maybe because of this, is monstrously powerful.

Speaking of the relationship between bodies-technologies-genders means
positioning oneself within the space of monstrosity and abjection. It means
dealing with everything that disturbs, distorts, rearticulates and makes visible the normative ties—which are generally taken for granted—between

---

24   Susan Stryker, "My Words to Victor Frankenstein Above the Village of Chamounix:
      Performing Transgender Rage," *GLQ* 1(3), 1994, pp. 237–54; Mary Shelley, *Frankenstein, or
      The Modern Prometheus*, 1817.

the biological specificity of the gender-differentiated human body, and the social roles and statuses that a particular body-conformity is predisposed to introject. This is a perspective that, in other words, highlights the subjectively-experienced dynamics between the perception of gender, social expectations correlated with it, and the cultural mechanisms that work to support or obstruct specific gendered configurations. Situating oneself within such a relationship points also to the possibility of a different understanding of "legitimate" meanings and representations of bodies: these are issues that initially seem theoretical but that, nevertheless, have concrete consequences for the conditions of livability.

Key to the work of boycotting the dualistic system of genders are new technologies, and material and discursive means for accessing the gender-scripts, and eliminating them.

The body reveals itself to be the space through which relations of power can be contested or confirmed, and in which symbolic and cultural meanings that individuals assign to their own bodies (and to others' bodies) conflict or are reaffirmed when they come in contact with the values and norms through which an entire society makes sense of bodies.

As De Lauretis and Balsamo teach us, one of the characteristics of gender is that it cannot be traced to any specific point on the body (genital organs, chromosomes, genes): it is spread throughout embodied subjects, materialized on and through them in a continuum of discourses, representations, practices and performances.[25]

Techno trans feminist experiences bring to light the indissolubility of the existing relationship between *soma*—the body, as an intelligible cultural construct—and *technè*—the technologies in and through which bodies take shape, transform and (re)position themselves. The transformational biotechnologies of the trans body, just like the apparatuses used in the production of pleasure for and through these same bodies, are not mere artificial "prostheses" installed on "natural" bodies but—and precisely because they are *bio*—they *are* the body itself. Ludovico Virtù's contribution moves in this direction when speaking of the sex toy industry; he stresses the subversive potential of self-organizing when it works within and for unconventional spaces, bodies, and identities. Paraphrasing his words, do-it-yourself becomes a potential way of recognizing the diversities of trans bodies, the spectrum of trans embodiment. Thus it is a formative practice, a way (mediated, but not immediate) to know

---

25   Teresa de Lauretis, *Technologies of Gender: Essays on Theory, Film and Fiction* (Bloomington: Indiana University Press, 1987); and Anne Balsamo, *Technologies of the Gendered Body: Reading Cyborg Women* (Durham: Duke University press, 1995).

and recognize alternative embodiment. Do-it-yourself is a journey of becoming, in which the epistemological linearity between an already known body and the production of objects that reflect the needs of such a body is broken in order to give life to a pathway of knowledge toward one's own body and one's own pleasures that emerge precisely through this do-it-yourself practice: making your own sex toys because your trans body isn't un/known, yet re/discovering the sensitivities of your own body through do-it-yourself production.[26]

The term *somatechnics* which was coined by Susan Stryker derives from this theoretical position—in which we may also trace some of the reflections already elaborated on by Donna Haraway—and is meant to indicate the strong link between the body and the technological apparatuses that form and transform bodies. It is precisely the dichotomy between the body and technology, nature and culture, that is definitively called into question: the body is not recognized as one, among many, (already given) known objects, but more so as *the* temporary space of what is understood, and a space for knowledge construction that assigns priority to processes of *embodiment* and subject position.

On the one hand, the "technologies of the body"[27] are the ways in which individuals in diverse societies know how to use their bodies, while on the other hand technologies that contemporary societies have access to include "the ways in which erotic bodies are [...] managed through medical or at least technical interventions."[28] In this transition we have a foundational shift in the body's perception of *de-gendered* experiences: from a biological body that is the bearer of a "natural" and uncontestable—and as such filled with problematics—sexual destiny, to a techno-modified body which is a platform for the experimentation of possibilities, of reinvention and (why not) a locus for the expression of happiness and euphoria.

Assuming that the body becomes a project[29] (whether individual or collective), means accepting that its character, its shape, its components are potentially subject to the desire for transformation, management and maintenance on the part of those who inhabit it, cross through it, hack it. In other words, we are talking about recognizing its importance as a personal resource and as a social symbol that transmits cultural, identitarian and collective meanings. In this context, each part of the body and each organ become malleable and

---

26   Ludovico Virtù, "Dis/organizing DIY Sexuality: A Trans Perspective," infra, 38-39.

27   Marcel Mauss M., *Le tecniche del corpo*, translated by Michel Fusaschi (Pisa: Edizioni ETS, 2017).

28   Ken Plummer, "La sociologia della sessualità e il ritorno del corpo," *Rassegna Italiana di Sociologia* 3, 2002, 496. (translation ours).

29   Chris Shilling, *The Body in Culture, Technology and Society* (London: SAGE, 2004).

mutable entities entrusted to their keepers, but also to larger socio-cultural systems, for surveillance and work.

The contributions in this collection tell us that techno trans feminist experiences are capable of revealing the workings of the systems and institutions that produce the possibility of livability for some subjects, while precluding it for others; they bring to light the problematic frameworks that determine the relationship between bodies and technologies (just think of the developments related to in vitro fertilization, organ transplants, and genetic engineering); they make ever more evident the ephemerality of the borders of bodies and their simultaneous ductility. Understanding the body as an economic resource in the current neoliberal context—precisely as a consequence of developments in biotechnology, and the pharmaceutical and pleasure industries— reveals new possibilities and new contradictions, starting with its being a locus of meaning-making and, at the same time, a social and cultural signifier.

The body—in being "molded and moldable on a social level"[30]—is marked by its intrinsic indeterminacy: it requires a continual negotiation of its own borders. For this reason, projects of body (self)transformation cannot be reduced to exercises of free personal choice, but rather, they presuppose negotiations with the social order that provide the systems of signification that are used to react, build, and give meaning to bodies.

In this journey, Paul Preciado's thinking is essential: for Preciado the body is a construction, a "field of multiplicity open to transformation,"[31] and the subject —that is always political—is the result of the implementation of precise technologies. Reflecting on the experience of the transformation of bodies and the modification of gender, Preciado interprets gender as a "political techno-economy," and its perception as a somato-political fiction produced by a set of technologies designed to domesticate the body.[32] He defines the contemporary sociopolitical context as a "pharmacopornographic regime," making reference to the processes of bio-molecular (pharmaco) and semiotic-technological (pornographic) management of the production of bodies and subjectivity. This context seems to be dominated by a series of technologies of the body (biotechnologies, surgery, endocrinology, pharmacology) and of representation (photography, cinema, television, cybernetics ...) which permeate daily life more than ever before. We are talking about biomolecular, digital, and high-speed information technologies: light, viscous, gelatinous, injectable,

---

30   Roberta Sassatelli, "Presentazione," *Rassegna italiana di sociologia* 3, 2002, 320.
31   Interview with Judith Butler and Paul B. Preciado, "Butler et Beatrice Preciado en Gran Entretien," *Têtu*, Dec 8th, 2009. www.tetu.com.
32   Paul B. Preciado, *Testo Junkie* (New York: Feminist Press, 2013).

inhalable, absorbable (one example is represented by gel testosterone and by its proliferation in the market). Preciado, along with Zygmunt Bauman, defines the contemporary sociopolitical context as being characterized by a sophisticated form of "liquid" control, but one could read it also as confessional, since "confession and pastoral power invert the process of individualization and control, opening the way for interrogation of liberal governmentality and biopolitics: in a feudal society, as is typical of sovereignty, the process of individualization is ascendant and primarily involves those with more power—those who will be more recognizable, more *individual*; in disciplinary societies, on the other hand, this process will be descendent, those with less power are more individualized, more visible."[33]

In the pharmacopornographic regime, bodies are not normed and disciplined by closing them within institutions, to the contrary, they seem to enjoy infinite freedom, which is possible because the "bland" technologies enact forms of micro-control, they worm their way into the bodies they aim to control, they become inseparable from them, they fuse together until becoming Subjectivity.

In the pharmacopornographic regime we embody the norm.

Gender ends up reincarnating itself in the body, giving life to a subjectivity that ossifies into identity with an extremely rigid taxonomy.

"None of the sexes that I embody has ontological density."[34]

The body is an invention. I produce and reproduce numerous "I"s; I embody them and at the same time none of them is me, none of them describes me completely. It is an expropriation that is not a loss, but rather a resource.

Preciado's analysis is interesting precisely because it is inserted within the neoliberal context in which the relationship between subjects and powers (whether they be medical, technological, apparatuses of control, etc.) is no longer circumscribable to the Foucauldian dialectic of resistance/control, but instead reveals a shift in perspective toward the complicity and negotiation of subjects. It is precisely this (re)active role that allows one to stress the necessity of the reappropriation of technologies of subjectivity production, through a direct involvement in the circulation and interpretation of "somato-politic biocodes."[35]

---

33   Carlotta Cossutta and Arianna Mainardi, "Surveillance, Subjectivity, and Public Space," infra, 115.

34   Interview with Butler and Preciado, *Têtu*, 2009.

35   Paul B. Preciado, *Testo Junkie*, 129.

The body, as it emerges from the words of the subjectivities that embody it, is thus not just a discursive effect,[36] but a real and true discursive agent, that plays a central and concrete role in the construction of the self, of gender, of sexuality, and of its position in public (when it comes to relationships and affects), and in virtual space. In the contributions in this volume, embodied subjectivities take on, manage, and modify individual and collective codes. The disidentification of the anatomy and the search for new identifications are processes that allow for the outlining of projects on the body that make the agency of subjects explicit. These processes also make it possible to consider the body a resource at its own disposal and not an error, a mistake, an obstacle in the way of bodily and gendered self-expressions. Technologies allow one to "see the possibility of another life,"[37] and produce a higher level of awareness and self-determination as they are techno trans feminist subjects. In conclusion, using Preciado's words once more, it is possible to affirm that "in terms of political agency, subjection, or empowerment do not depend on the rejection of technologies in the name of nature, but rather on the differential use and reappropriation of the very techniques of the production of subjectivity."[38]

Even this reappropriation, however, is full of complexity and risks, as Donna Haraway warned us twenty years ago, in a text that is unfortunately out of print in Italy, but continues to circulate almost clandestinely: "More than a little amnesiac about how colonial travel narratives work, we peered inside our vaginas toward the distant cervix and said something like, 'Land ho!' We have discovered ourselves and claim the new territory for women. In the context of the whole orthodox history of Western philosophy and technology—visual self-possessed sexual and generative organs made potent tropes for the reclaimed feminist self. We thought we had our eyes on the prize."[39] Haraway also assertively returns in the various contributions of this text because her reflection on the interconnection between bodies and technologies is both critical and a subversive reappropriation. Haraway repeatedly reminds us that

---

36   See also: Michel Foucault, *The History of Sexuality, Volume I* (New York: Random House, 1978); and Judith Butler, *Gender Trouble. Feminism and Subversion of Identity* (New York: Routledge, 1990).

37   Paul B. Preciado, *Testo Junkie*, 367.

38   Ibid., 129.

39   Donna Haraway, *Modest_Witness@Second_Millenium.FemaleMan_Meets_OncoMouse* (New York: Routledge, 1997) 193. Hawarway does not forget, however, the practical importance of movement for women's health: "those collective sessions with the speculum and mirror were not only symbols, however. They were self-help and self-experimentation practices in a period in which abortion was still illegal and unsafe." Donna Haraway, *Modest_Witness*, 193.

technologies are a tool, with a story, an imaginary, and a function, just like all other tools, that do not exhaust the horizon of change, even if they may help reach it: for example "the fullest meanings of reproductive freedom critical to feminist technoscience politics cannot easily be signified by the gynecological speculum or by the virtual speculum of the computer terminal, no matter how important it remains to control, inhabit, and shape those tools, both semiotically and materially."[40]

Echography is a technology that Haraway spends some time on, it marks a point of passage in a process of change in the borders of the body and in the distinction between inside and outside. Furthermore, the sonogram shows the encounter between the patriarchy and biopolitics as a technology that, from the very beginning, primarily inspects women's wombs, in a process of medicalizing pregnancy that runs parallel to the need to produce healthy populations.[41] The invention of the sonogram comes from military developments in radar, and was used first and foremost in psychiatry to observe the brain, but with poor results because of the cranium's thickness; then it was used to observe pregnancies, becoming, in a very short time, a widely-used exam. The proximity between military research and uterine observation already tells us a lot about a colonial connection assigned to bodies that defines the possibilities of their understanding.

In 1965 *Life* magazine dedicated a cover to "an unprecedented photographic feat in color:"[42] the images represent a 17-week-old live fetus in its amniotic sac. The article accompanying the photograph of the fetus tells of the journey of the spermatozoa and the insemination of the egg in a very narrative way, in a story that assigns the active role of the conquering male to the spermatozoa, and the passive role of the conquered female to the egg: this will prove to be a popular story, but it also shows how the images alone are still incomprehensible without the help of an expert's eye, like that of a doctor. Haraway maintains that "The sonogram is literally a pedagogy for learning to see who exists in the world. Selves and subjects are produced in such 'lived experiences.'"[43] The sonogram, therefore, isn't just a useful medical tool, it is an indicator of a new life, a standardized mode of turning the product of a pregnancy into a subject. Barbara Duden shares a conversation with her colleague,

---

40　Ibid., 196–7.

41　We, the translators of this volume, want to acknowledge the problematic nature of the use of the term "women" in this context. Not all women have wombs, and many who are not women-identified have wombs.

42　"Drama of Life Before Birth," *Life*, April 30th, 1965, cover.

43　Ibid., 177.

Joanne, who tells of being pregnant and showing polaroids of her sonogram to her friends one Sunday afternoon. Joanne recalls: "In the image, I could make out a cloudlike pattern in three or four shades of gray." In this blurred image Joanne recognized her son John. This simple image, however, is not as peaceful as it might appear: Joanne is divorced, far from home, and she wouldn't have wanted a second child, but she affirms that "since I know that it's human, that it belongs to me, that it moves, I could not think of an abortion."[44] Seeing the fetus, being able to show it to friends, makes it real, alive and present in a much stronger way than merely knowing it is in the body, as if seeing it gives life to the fetus. Donna Haraway emphasizes that "It does not seem too much to claim that the biomedical, public fetus—given flesh by the high technology of visualization—is a sacred-secular incarnation, the material realization of the promise of life itself. Here is the fusion of art, science, and creation. No wonder we look."[45]

This power to visualize can also be deployed as *anti-abortionist*, as is evidenced by the video *The Silent Scream* that seeks to show, through ultrasonic images, the abortion of a twenty-week-old fetus.[46] What stands out, first and foremost, is the power of the fetal image and the acceptance of this image as an accurate representation of a real fetus. This power derives from the particular ability of images to assume empirical, informative and mythic meaning. In *The Silent Scream* the fetus that we see and recognize is nothing more than a fetish: in fact, it is shown from the point of view of the camera and not of the pregnant woman or the fetus itself, despite the fact that the video's narrator describes it as "the perspective of the victim." The fetus has become a kind of alien, suspended in space, and a part of both science fiction and the popular imaginary. Because the fetus is always represented from the perspective of the male spectator, women's perception of her own fetus is also filtered through this male lens.[47]

In *The Silent Scream* the fictional image, provided by the video, merges with clinical biotechnics using medical language that works in the service of patriarchal messages. The images of the video confuse the border between fetus

---

44   Barbara Duden, *Disembodying Women: Perspectives on Pregnancy and the Unborn* (Cambridge: Harvard University Press, 1993) 31.

45   Donna Haraway, *Modest_Witness*, 179.

46   The 1984 American video on abortion filmed and directed by Dr. Bernard Nathanson. The video shows the details of the abortion of a twenty-week-old fetus (www.silentscream.org).

47   The use of the term "woman" here is a nod to Laura Mulvey and second wave feminist theory, but we want to specify that the experience of pregnancy is filtered through this male lens of regardless the gender identity of the subject.

and child, they reinforce the idea that the identity of the fetus is separate and autonomous from the mother, as is evidenced by the near total absence of the woman in the video. The spectator is encouraged to identify with the fetus as subject, aside from, if not through, the exclusion of the mother. Thus, the video becomes an extreme example of how visual obstetric technologies and other forms of medical intervention break down the traditional *internal/external* dichotomy used to conceive of many things, including the ways we understand women's bodies. This dismantling, that the sonogram so efficiently depicts, is definitely dangerous when used for patriarchal ends.

But some previously unforeseen possibilities are opened for the subversion and contamination of the notion of an unchanging biological nature. The concept of nature, in fact, has always been a prison in which to enclose women and all those subjectivities that lie outside the social norms that are sold as natural. Technological skill, to the contrary, can become an escape or even an enjoyment. Once again, it is Haraway who emphasizes how "intense pleasure in skill, machine skill, ceases to be a sin, but an aspect of embodiment. The machine is not an it to be animated, worshiped, and dominated. The machine is us, our processes, an aspect of our embodiment."[48] Skill, in this sense, allows one to escape a dimension of the body that is understood as destiny, and to brush against the borders between natural and artificial, to always be out of place, neither fully human, nor fully machine: cyborg, in all forms that we can imagine.

As Elisa Virgili brings to light, "[b]ody and technology have never been this hybrid, the border between the single body, the collective, and digital technologies is fragmented to produce resistance."[49] Thus, bodies become porous, and the artificiality of sexual and gender distinctions becomes clearer because we can modify them with various technologies. But, bodies carry with them the history of their oppressions and, as Lucía Egaña Rojas puts it, "The body has memory; one needn't go too far. A transfeminist technology carries carved in its flesh the imprisonment of Angela Davis, the witch hunts, the trans people dead at every border, in their homes. [...] Technology is material. It is not an abstraction. In Silicon Valley, broadband passes over the rooftops of the *maquiladoras*. Technology is a geological fact, made up of layers that create structural patterns that begin with cataclysm, scars and golden showers."[50] Not only does technology allow us to rethink our bodies, but bodies themselves emphasize the materiality of technology, of its history, of its uses. Angela Balzano, for

---

48   Donna Haraway, *Cyborg Manifesto*, 180.
49   Elisa Virgili, "If I Was a Rich Girl," infra, 69.
50   Lucía Egaña Rojas, "Technofeminism," infra, 29.

example, shows us the dark sides of reproductive technologies, that reify the desires for parenthood and end up catering only to potential mothers: "In this way, the rhetoric of the sacredness of reproduction resurfaces, even in the era of the intersection between technological apparatuses and bio-tech markets; but, as it surpasses nature in the name of the miracle of life, insisting exclusively on the "dream of motherhood," isn't it using new tools to re-present us with the old existential recipe of wife-mother?"[51]

This emphasis on bodies and their positionality is fundamental for not succumbing to the temptation of seeing utopias in already existing technologies.

The interwoven relationship between technology's ability to be transformative but also normativizing pervades, not just this text, but all theory linking technology to bodies, genders, and sexualities. This scholarship depends on our paying vigilant attention to structures of power that create technology, the social imaginary around its use, and the material conditions that make it possible. The challenge, thus, is to not look away from the dark sides of digital screens; the challenge is to try to take them apart or inhabit them without any illusion of progress that would necessarily lead to better fate. Or, to say it as Valerie Solanas in *SCUM* says it, keeping in mind "[t]he male changes only when forced to do so by technology, when he has no choice, when 'society' reaches the stage where he must change or die. We're at this stage now; if women don't get their asses in gear fast, we may very well all die."[52] In other words, society changes only if the relations of subordination change, and this must start with oppressed and excluded subjectivities, it must start with the margins, from the sweaters off their backs: from the fissures.

Of course, "[o]ur relations to place, like our relations to people, are studded with bias, riven with contradictions, and complicated by opaque emotional responses,"[53] we don't avoid pain, we don't want to be heroines, we cross through it. Our body-spaces are vulnerable, we protect them, we refuse them, we dress them, we undress them, we occupy them, we leave them. It is precisely in this explosion of pluralities, which is negated by heteronormativity, that the queer transfeminist resides.

Laboria Cuboniks writes: "Intervention in more obviously material hegemonies is just as crucial as intervention in digital and cultural ones. Changes to the built environment harbor some of the most significant possibilities in the reconfiguration of the horizons of women and queers. As the embodiment of

51   Angela Balzano, "Virtual Interfaces of Biotech Reproduction," infra, 50-51.

52   Valerie Solanas, *SCUM Manifesto*, (London: The Olympia Press, 1971) 24.

53   Jack Halberstam, *In A Queer Time and Place: Transgender Bodies, Subcultural Lives*, (New York: New York University Press, 2005) 22.

FIGURE 1.5   "Electric sunsets"
           PHOTO BY CARLOTTA COSSUTTA

ideological constellations, the production of space and the decisions we make for its organization are ultimately articulations about 'us' and reciprocally, how a 'we' can be articulated."[54]

Lucía Egaña Rojas adds: "A transfeminist technology will, in the same way, try to overcome vulnerability in the public space of the technomechanical internet. Google is not a safe space. Its servers are enrolled in the list of tools necessary to heteropatriarchal discourse; tools kept in an armored vault. We can come and go from these serves (and more often than not they push us out, not explaining why they are forcing us to leave) because, in some ways, we have always lived in insecure spaces, building forts of collective and affective protection. But I am asking for a transfeminist technology that creates its own safe spaces, in cities and on the web. I am asking for free serves, without censorship,

---

54   Laboria Cuboniks, *Xenofeminism.*

in which we do not need to dissimulate our content, or self-censor our videos. I am asking that we organize so as to achieve this."[55]

Things are complicated, and to understand them, to explain them, to inhabit them, what we need is complex thought that is not consolatory.

A stupendous thought.

Works Cited

Balsamo, Anne. *Technologies of the Gendered Body: Reading Cyborg Women*. Durham (NC): Duke University Press, 1995.

Butler, Judith. *Gender Trouble. Feminism and Subversion of Identity*. New York: Routledge, 1990.

Casalini, Brunella and Federico Zappino. "Preface." In *Corpi 2.0. Sulla dilatabilità tecnica dell'Uomo*, 6–11. Edited by Karin Harrasser. Florence: goWare, 2018.

Cuboniks, Laboria. *Xenofeminism*. https://laboriacuboniks.net/manifesto/.

De Lauretis, Teresa. *Technologies of Gender: Essays on Theory, Film, and Fiction*. Bloomington: Indiana University Press, 1987.

Duden, Barbara. *Disembodying Women: Perspectives on Pregnancy and the Unborn*. Cambridge: Harvard University Press, 1993.

Foucault, Michel. *The History of Sexuality, Volume I*. Paris: Random House, 1978.

Gajjala, Radhika and Yeon Ju Oh. *Cyberfeminism 2.0*. New York: Peter Lang Publishing, 2012.

Gilman, Charlotte Perkins. *The Home: Its Work and Influence*. New York: McClure, Phillips, & Co., 1903.

Halberstam, Jack. *In A Queer Time and Place: Transgender Bodies, Subcultural Lives*. New York: New York University Press, 2005.

Haraway, Donna. *Modest_Witness@Second_Millenium.FemaleMan_Meets_OncoMouse*. New York: Routledge, 1997.

Haraway, Donna. *Simians, Cyborgs and Women: The Reinvention of Nature*. New York: Routledge, 1991.

Haraway, Donna. "Situated Knowledges: The Science Question in Feminism and the Privilege of Partial Perspective." *Feminist Studies* 14, no. 3 (1998): 575–99.

Kember, Sarah and Joanna Zylinska. *Life After New Media: Mediation as a Vital Process*. Boston: MIT Press, 2012.

Lakoff, George and Mark Johnson. *Metaphors We Live By*. Chicago: University of Chicago Press, 1980.

---

55   Lucía Egaña Rojas, "Technofeminism," infra, 30.

Leurs, Koen. "Performing Gender and Ethnicity in Socio-Technological Networks: Entangling Feminist Technoscience and Postcolonial Studies." *International Journal of Feminist Technoscience*. 2009.

Mauss, Marcel M. *Le tecniche del corpo*. Translated by Michel Fusaschi. Pisa: Edizioni ETS, 2017.

Murray, Janet H. *Hamlet on the Holodeck: The Future of Narrative in Cyberspace*. New York: Simon and Schuster, 1997.

Plummer, Ken. "La sociologia della sessualità e il ritorno del corpo." *Rassegna Italiana di Sociologia* 3 (2002): 496.

Preciado, Paul B. "La tecnologia cambia i corpi e le coscienze." *Internazionale*. Internazionale, January 30, 2017. https://www.internazionale.it/opinione/paul-preciado/2017/01/30/tecnologia-corpi-coscienze.

Preciado, Paul B. *Testo Junkie. Sex, Drugs and Biopolitics in the Pharmacopornographic Era*. New York: Feminist Press, 2013.

Sassatelli, Roberta. "Presentazione." *Rassegna Italiana di Sociologia* 3 (2002): 320.

Shilling, Chris. *The Body in Culture, Technology and Society*. London: SAGE, 2004.

Solanas, Valerie. *SCUM Manifesto*. London: The Olympia Press, 1971.

Stryker, Susan. "My Words to Victor Frankenstein Above the Village of Chamounix: Performing Transgender Rage." *GLQ* 1, no. 3 (1994): 237–54.

Wajcman, Judy. "From Women and Technology to Gendered Technoscience Information." *Community and Society* 10, no. 3 (2007): 287–98.

CHAPTER 2

Technofeminism

Notes for a Transfeminist Technology (Version 3.0)

Lucía Egaña Rojas

> root@root: I am speaking from the precarity of the machines, from a place transformed by error. I speak as a pornWorker of code, as a pariah. I speak from the smartphone I bought with my first wages as a prostitute; I use OpenOffice to write love letters to a hacker I don't know. I speak through videochat, I use Anglicisms and I use them poorly. Technology and science are two words wrested carelessly from the same definition in the dictionary. I speak with this language that is mediated by computers and online dictionaries. The online dictionary gushes from my mouth. Technophilia and Technophobia are two forces battling within me. They are like vaginal bacteria, the danger lies in their losing their balance (in that case I use kefir to restore order). I am speaking as a spammer, a steamer, a blogger and a switcher.
>
> *PornoObreros del codigo* (PornWorkers of Code)[1]

∴

Margarita Padilla recounts the moment in which, for the first time, she wanted to become a hacker.[2] After attending a conference that had fascinated her, she begins to fantasize about the possibility of presenting the following year. When she gets home, she notices the hallway is dirty. So, she thinks: "If I go on GNOME, who will clean the hallway?"[3]

---

1 Lucía Egaña Rojas, "PornoObreros del código," *La categoría del porno*, exhibition, curated by Felipe Rivas San Martin, (Biblioteca de Santiago, Sala+18: Santiago de Chile 2012).

2 An earlier version of this was published in *Transfeminismos. Epistemes, fricciones e flujos,* ed.s Miriam Solà, Elena Urko, (Txalaparta: Tafalla, 2013).

3 Semi-unedited material taken from an interview with Margarita Padilla in November of 2010. LelaCoders. "Margarita," October 19, 2011, video, https://vimeo.com/30812111.

It is hard to write in the face of household chores or the yoke of multi-tasking; two of the many ways of dispossessing ourselves of writing tools;[4] another obstacle is writing's singular, correct definition. Spelling, methodology, category and order. Diction and science. Complete dedication to one thing, specialization and professionalism. In the shower I think about writing as a technology of definitions (I hadn't interviewed Padilla yet). What should the discursive methods of transfeminism be? Soap. Feminist writing should include blogs, performances, government statements, scratches and tattoos, and vaginal lesions (prosthetic lesions) in addition to texts. "Writing is preeminently the technology of cyborgs, etched surfaces of the late twentieth century. Cyborg politics is the struggle for language and the struggle against perfect communication, against the one code that translates all meaning perfectly, the central dogma of phallogocentrism."[5]

"Writing becomes a privileged operating table where anatomy can be operated on with sexuo-political definitions of the body, short circuiting the technologies of production of somatic fictions, unsettling the state, the church, the capital, science and their industries."[6]

The common definition of technology suggests a division between the environment and the one who owns or creates technology, a difference between natural and artificial. An antagonism between the two parts, a struggle for power. The common definition of technology presupposes a scientific organization of knowledge, a progressive viewpoint oriented towards the industrialization of technology for economic gain.

Audre Lorde held a conference at New York University in 1984, at which she denounced how the technologies of race and sexual orientation had structured the only discursive possibilities. "The master's tools will never dismantle the master's house."[7] By "tools" Lorde means the labels of "feminist, lesbian

---

4   In 1843 Ada Lovelace writes a contract for Charles Babbage: "undertake to give your mind *wholly and undividedly*, as a primary object that no engagement is to interfere with, to the consideration of all those matters in which I shall at times require your intellectual *assistance & supervision*; & can you promise not to *slur & hurry* things over; or to mislay & allow confusion & mistakes to enter into documents &c?" [from Doris Langley Moore, *Ada, Countess of Lovelace, Byron's Illegitimate Daughter*. London: John Murray, 1997, p. 171; in Sadie Plant, "The Future Looms: Weaving Women and Cybernetics," *Body and Society, v.1 (3–4)*, p. 47].

5   Donna Haraway, *Simians, Cyborgs, and Women*, (Routledge: New York, 1991), p. 176.

6   Valeria Flores, *Industrias del cuerpo. Ficciones feministas, fábulas epistemológicas y políticas del desacato*. Text presented at the Third Circuit of Sexual Dissidence "There's No Respect," organized by the University Coordinator for Sexual Dissidence (Cuds), Santiago, Chile June 2011, p. 9.

7   Audre Lorde, "The Master's Tools Will Never Dismantle the Master's House," in *Sister Outsider*, (Berkeley: Crossing Press: 1984), 110–114.

and black" which in feminism (beginning from a place of good intention, of wanting to give visibility to the conditions of experience), provoked a division of categories that prevented her from referring to aspects of her life that lie outside her condition as feminist, lesbian and black.

A condition mutilated by a techno-knife, by the dust in the hallway, by some soap in the academic program of feminist visibility. Because "every person is formed (controlled) by specific social technologies that define them in terms of gender, social class, race."[8]

What would a transfeminist technology be like, how would it be defined, what would its use be? How can we talk about technology when we know that the social construction of sex and gender passes through closed source programming and that, even if we open it, if we free it and make it explicit, the majority of the open code will close itself again because of the barbarity of industrialization, because of the desire to get married, because of fashion, hospitals, prison? "Technofeminism" is the space described in a dystopian science fiction novel that we have been acting out for more than fifteen years. In this novel, "Bodies are screens on which we see projected the momentary settlements that emerge from ongoing struggles over beliefs and practices within the academic and medical communities."[9]

This novel also tells a story of resistance.

Following are the descriptions, in no particular order, of a few scenes.

1   **Artifacts and Abilities**

In the world of technology the "dicksize war" is so common a thing that it has become normalized (just like the passion for results). It doesn't matter what you do with your dick in the dicksize war, how big it is or how long it takes to get hard. Efficiency and presence. Speed. In this competition only dicks matter, "flesh" ones (only gadgets, artifacts, devices, machines, only things that have integrated circuits, a cpu, a computer code). In this war empowerment seems to coincide with ego. Processes, observations, narratives and senses don't count in the dicksize war. It is a dynamic that is reifying and material, and is the result of an unusual technological essentialism.[10]

---

8   Post-OP "Plataforma de investigacion de genero y post-pornografia," *Postporno Blogspot* (Blog) Collective Commons Publishing. Postporno.blogspot.com.

9   Sandy Stone, *The "Empire" Strikes Back: A Posttransexual Manifesto*, (Austin: University of Texas, 1993), p. 11. https://uberty.org/wp-content/uploads/2015/06/trans-manifesto.pdf.

10   In 2012, during the LabSurLab held in Quito, at the panel dedicated to gender and technology, a few members of Corpanp (Corporación de productores audiovisuales de las

The dicksize war is, as the name suggests, a parade of reified abilities during which one of those on display will win (and the odds of "winning" go up with the latest model machine, with access to private property, and with a very intimate relationship to the traditional definition of technology).

The dicksize war is not a useful methodology for learning so much as it is for observing things. It is a dynamic based on ownership and public recognition ("look how beautiful my tool is"); that's why, in the dystopian science fiction novel, this scene describes a sort of primitive, hegemonic state.

This is an antecedent that justifies the emergence of new cyborg characters, of emancipated machines and multiple short circuits that will create a new species of tecnoScum commanders.

2   The Cloud

Capitalist technology is oriented toward the loss of autonomy and self-determination. The contemporaneous interfaces and operating systems work like black boxes for the processes that take place inside them. The internet is visualized as a "cloud," and the devices connected to it by way of invisible, immaterial cables, transmit performances of identity that are easy to catalog and are always orderly.

Capitalism serially produces the need for repetition because it needs (and produces) the routine and the factory.

The only difference between one product and another is its serial number, a thing that, paradoxically, gives it its "originality."

In capitalism the action is completed at the point of consumption, and liberty is translated as the possibility of choice in a limited range of products and alternatives.

An anticapitalist technology does not have serial numbers, nor does it have factories, nor does it have euphemisms about clouds.[11]

An anticapitalist technology is not in the clouds, nor is it made in China; because it is, among other places, in the rebel cunt that resists pantyliners as

---

nacionalidades y pueblos; Corporation of Audiovisual Producers of Nations and Peoples) declared that their knowledge of technology is millenary. One needs to be able to observe the river beds and the cycles of the moon to know when to plant seeds, one needs to be able to listen to the earth and respond to the vital rhythms. These types of technologies, obviously, wouldn't qualify you for a cock fight.

11   The 1999 ad campaign for the Evax pantyliner had, as its slogan, the question "What do clouds smell like?" http://www.youtube.com/watch?v=d-p8FxFS1_M (visited March 2013).

the paradigm of castrating homogenization (and here the olfactory technologies proposed by Tampax are one of the tools of the industry).

An anticapitalist technology will be transfeminist because it will not be in the clouds, because when the code is opened the subtle engineering of monogamy as the production of guilt will become visible, Chinese finger-traps, x-rays and predetermined roles will be revealed.

In the dominant culture, the default operating system is Windows; sexuality is, by default, white, monogamous, singleparent; habit is a niche market; but when codes are open none of this is credible because it seems so "original" as to appear boring, at the very least. The repetition is boring. A transfeminist technology is based on the unrepeatability of each small gesture, on serendipity and chance.

3   Illiterate

Can we imagine a person illiterate in the technologies of gender? A person who uses devices poorly, who mispronounces her ID, who has never learned?

Illiteracy is a condition of poverty; there is a relationship between limited access to technology and marginalization.

A transfeminist technology would value illiteracy in its function as an unproductive industry, as a way of following unthought pathways towards productivity and speed, as a mode of resistance.

Rather than an illness, aphasia would become a way of developing new languages.

Traditional methods presuppose a search for disembodied results that, in all the questions and hypotheses, ends up destroying that which had been vital to the object of study.

Experience and the body, just like privacy, are elements that must be excluded from this research (and from technological action) because, in this way, the abject can be made to be condition-free, and the codes can remain distant from the construction of subjectivity.

"A queer methodology, in a way, is a scavenger methodology that uses different methods to collect and produce information on subjects who have been deliberately or accidentally excluded from traditional studies of human behavior. The queer methodology attempts to combine methods that are often cast as being at odds with each other, and it refuses the academic compulsion toward disciplinary coherence."[12]

---

12   Jack Halberstam, *Female Masculinity*, (Duke University Press: Durham, NC, 1998) p.13.

A transfeminist relationship with technology can't help but give visibility to the space of subjectivity and the body, because therein lie the elements at the center of power and hierarchy. Technofeminism will discover languages and paths to learning that do not simply give technologies a blank slate; instead, if the technologies don't work, they will make them function permanently, or they will create effects capable of deconstructing the original machinery of the system.

A series of knowledges that are both unregulated and, likely, not approved by the sciences. A contagious pedagogy that operates by way of incarnation, an anti-pedagogy, because it will never be recognized as such, because it works on biography and life, and because this type of anti-pedagogy is one of the most powerful tools for creating networks of resistance, for the contagion of the subjective, and the abandonment of the outdated "I."

4   Geology, Body and Matter

Why do we need a powerful computer when, more than thirty years ago, Foucault left us a toolbox that we continue to use today? Why did I whore myself out for a smartphone?

As Gayle Rubin writes, "In geological time the present is a blip [...] the infrastructures of knowledge require physical space and durable organizational structures."[13] Does it have to do with hacklabs, libraries, bodies?

We must find the origins, the code, not just in the software, but also in history, in the imposed machines, in the cultural backbone and institutional censorship.

Technology needs memory, it needs to know the origins of every scar. It needs bridges, translators, archivists. It needs the weight of documentation to exceed the feminine sphere of care in order to protect new forms of memory and action.

The body has memory; one needn't go too far. A transfeminist technology carries carved in its flesh the imprisonment of Angela Davis, the witch hunts, the trans people dead at every border, in their homes. A transtechnofeminist body knows injustice and violation, it knows and lives with the precarity of machines (that are in its body). The cyborg body should be understood as a marked body, a body marked by the struggles of class, xenophobia and racism.

---

13   Gayle Rubin, *Deviations: A Gayle Rubin Reader*, (Duke University Press: Durham, NC, 2011), p. 335.

Technology is material. It is not an abstraction. In the Silicon Valley, broadband passes over the rooftops of the *maquiladoras*.[14] Technology is a geological fact, made up of layers that create structural patterns that begin with cataclysm, scars and golden showers.

They made us believe technology is a software, immaterial and intangible, but "eat code and die [...] We are the malignant accident which fell into your system while you were sleeping. And when you wake we will terminate your digital delusions, hijacking your impeccable software."[15] It is not enough to revindicate history, we must also take back memory. We must look for ways of disseminating and establishing viral cyborgs,[16] because a cyborg isn't just an aesthetic, it is also, and above all, a painful experience, painful on account of the materiality of technology.

5   Fear

A transfeminist technology creates safe spaces that, in theory, are already established at parties, meetings, after-parties. A transfeminist technology will, in the same way, try to overcome vulnerability in the public space of the technomechanical internet. Google is not a safe space. Its servers are enrolled in the list of tools necessary for heteropatriarchal discourse; tools kept in an armored vault. We can come and go from these servers (and more often than not they push us out, not explaining why they are forcing us to leave) because, in some ways, we have always lived in insecure spaces, building forts of collective and affective protection. But I am asking for a transfeminist technology that creates its own safe spaces, in cities and on the web. I am asking for free servers,

---

14   A *maquiladora* is a term for a foreign-owned factory in Mexico that makes use of cheap labor to assemble products for export.

15   VNS Matrix, *Bitch Mutant Manifesto,* 1996. https://vnsmatrix.net/projects/bitch-mutant -manifesto.

16   In fact, cyborg knowledge should be understood as something completely different from that which reproduces the dominant global order; therefore, cyborg consciousness needs to be developed with a series of technologies that, when united, constitute the methodology of the oppressed, a methodology oriented toward survival and resistance of the transnational cultural conditions of the First World. This oppositional "cyborg" knowledge has been assimilated with terms like "mimetic knowledge," "situated subjectivities," "feminism" and "differential knowledge" [Chela Sandoval, "New Sciences. Cyborg Feminism and the Methodology of the Oppressed," *The Cyborg Handbook,* ed. C. Grey, (London: Routledge, 1995), 407–422].

without censorship, in which we do not need to dissimulate our content, or self-censor[17] our videos. I am asking that we organize so as to achieve this.

A transfeminist technology is not afraid of machines, or of body self-exploration, to learn what's inside; in the cervix and beyond. A transfeminist technology will be a collective practice and a systematic shedding of fear; a study to learn how the cables are connected (cultural or mechanical) within the boxes represented by our bodies or laptops. In the Eighties, Sandy Stone built herself a computer and programmed it. A transfeminist technology will make fun of the obsolete practice of programming the body in order to render obsolete the practice of programming gender; at the same time, it will fondle machines, and reuse the pieces, it will know how to open laptops and recognize anal pleasure.

I am asking that we explore artisanal technologies, without patents, the technologies of horror, hacking, technologies of dissidence, low-key technologies. Social technologies, of abject genders and of countercultures. I am asking–with a desperate scream ignited by Haraway–for writing codes to be fearlessly extracted, to open the machines and to never again shed a tear over a dead computer.

(The modem is already between my legs).[18]

Works Cited

Egaña Rojas, Lucia. "PornoObreros del código." *La categoría del porno*, exhibition, curated by Felipe Rivas San Martin. Biblioteca de Santiago, Sala+18: Santiago de Chile 2012.

Flores, Valeria. "Industrias del cuerpo. Ficciones feministas, fábulas epistemológicas y políticas del desacato." Text presented at the Third Circuit of Sexual Dissidence "There's No Respect," Santiago, Chile, June 2011.

Halberstam, Jack. *Female Masculinity*. Durham (NC): Duke University Press, 1998.

Haraway, Donna. *Simians, Cyborgs, and Women.* New York: Routledge, 1991.

Lorde, Audre. *Sister Outsider: Essays and Speeches.* Berkeley, CA: Crossing Press, 2007.

---

17   See also an interview in which Pier Paolo Pasolini talks about mass media, alluding precisely to the fact that the device of television operates on implicit self-censorship that he himself exerts in the act of speaking in that context, in addition to censorship being a hierarchy constructed by the device itself. *Pasolini on Mass Television*, undated interview (www.youtube.come/watch?v=FCM1x0pkiOM, visited March 2013).

18   VSN Matrix, 1996.

Moore, Doris Langley. *Ada, Countess of Lovelace, Byron's Illegitimate Daughter.* London: John Murray, 1997.

Plant, Sadie. "The Future Looms: Weaving Women and Cybernetics." *Body and Society* 1, no. 3–4 (1995): 47.

Rubin, Gayle. *Deviations: A Gayle Rubin Reader.* Durham (NC): Duke University Press, 2011.

Sandoval, Chela. "New Sciences. Cyborg Feminism and the Methodology of the Oppressed." In *The Cyborg Handbook.* Edited by C. Grey, 407–422. London: Routledge, 1995.

Solà, Miriam and Elena Urko. *Transfeminisms. Epistemes, frictions and flows.* Tafalla: Txalaparta, 2013.

Stone, Sandy. *The 'Empire' Strikes Back: A Posttransexual Manifesto.* Austin: University of Texas, 1993. https://uberty.org/wp-content/uploads/2015/06/trans-manifesto.pdf.

VNS Matrix. *Bitch Mutant Manifesto.* 1996. https://vnsmatrix.net/projects/bitch-mutant-manifesto.

CHAPTER 3

Dis/Organizing D-I-Y Sexuality

A Trans Perspective

Ludovico Virtù

1 Trans and Sexuality, a Silent Intersection

In my research on the sex toy industry I have tried to understand how the production of sex toys works, or rather, what kinds of practices and organizational discourses develop in such a context.[1] I was curious in particular, about how the production of sex toys–which for a long time was considered unlawful, perverse, queer–in the last twenty years turned into a real industry targeted at "whomever," women and men, straights and gays, wants to experiment by themselves or in couples. Through the course of my research I often asked myself if and how, in the context of the capitalization of sexuality, the critical potentiality that these technologies have in terms of spaces, bodies, and non-conventional identities could still emerge, and if this could be separated from the idea of profit.

In 2016 I happened upon a workshop on do-it-yourself sex toys in a trans and non-binary culture festival in a mid-sized city in Northern Europe. The aim of this festival, which was organized by a trans association,[2] was to establish a free program made up of workshops, film screenings, debates and presentations on sexuality, gender, identity categories, and the versatile space that exists (and that can exist) within and beyond such categories and identities. With the participation of activists who identify as both trans and cis,[3] the festival wants to take on themes of sex, kink practices,[4] relationships and desires,

---

1 Virtù expanded upon themes in this chapter in "Displacing the Gender Binary Through Modes of Dis/organizing: Sex Toys, Sexuality and Trans Politics," *Politics and Governance*, 8, no.3 (2020): 321–331.

2 I have deliberately chosen to leave out the details of the name of the association out of respect for the privacy of those participating in my research, who, in my analyses appear under pseudonyms.

3 Cis, or cisgender refers to those people who do not identify as trans or transgender and/or live the gender they were assigned at birth. See: Julia Serano, *Whipping Girl: A Transsexual Woman on Sexism and the Scapegoating of Femininity* (Berkeley: Seal Press, 2007); Susan Stryker, *Transgender History: The Roots of Today's Revolution,* (Berkeley: Seal Press, 2008).

4 Kink refers to non-conventional sexual, erotic and bdsm practices (bondage, discipline, domination, submission, sadism, and masochism), fetish and the use of sex toys.

and celebrate the "disorder" of identities and experiences of gender. In particular, the objective of the workshop on do-it-yourself sex toys was to carve out a space for discussion about sexuality that centralized trans, non-binary, and queer voices. The point of departure for those organizing was realizing the difficulty (not to mention reticence) in tracking down those interested in dealing with the theme of sexuality in relation to the experiences, bodies, and identities of trans and non-binary people. Talking about sexuality and sexual practices that include objects and technologies like sex toys is still often taboo; to speak of them in relation to, and at the intersection of, trans experience is further marginalized and stigmatized, and rarely dealt with from a perspective of empowerment.[5] In the theoretical field, even trans scholars often avoid the subject, perhaps to distance themselves from a (cis-sexist) uninformed discourse that continues to consider trans experience a sexual orientation, or a dysfunction, instead of an identity/gender experience.[6] These discourses may also reinforce a transphobic and transmisogynist imaginary that hypersexualizes and/or fetishizes trans people, especially trans women and trans feminine people.[7] Yet, it is precisely by avoiding speaking about sexuality from a trans perspective that we run the risk of validating the lack of a self-produced sociocultural imaginary (an alternative to the cis-hetero-patriarchal one): the only one that is truly capable of allowing trans people to recognize themselves and be recognized as desiring and desirable subjects.[8]

Intending to contribute to a critical extension of this activist and academic debate (if it is possible to separate the two), I wanted to reflect first and foremost on the organizational aspect of this endeavor, or rather, on the processes of creating a space in which it is possible to explore the intersection between sexuality and trans experiences. In this article, I conceptualize this work as a "trans-organizing modality." What characterizes a trans-organizing modality on sexuality? What is called into question by a trans-organizing modality in this context? In other words: what impact does a trans-organizing modality have on existing conceptions of sexuality? To answer these questions, I decided to analyze the above-cited workshop on do-it-yourself sex toys as

5 Sade Kondelin, "Dis/Orientations of Gender and Sexuality in Transgender Embodiment," *SQS-Suomen Queer-tutkimuksen Seuran lehti* 8, no. 1–2 (2014): 32–43.

6 Clark Pignedoli, "Beyond Trans Medicalization: Gatekeeping and the Epistemological Privilege of Ignorance," (Paper presented at Cirque, Centro interuniversitario di recerca queer: L'Aquila, 2017).

7 Serano, *Whipping Girl*, 2007.

8 Gayle Salamon, *Assuming a Body: Transgender and Rhetorics of Materiality*, (New York: Columbia University Press, 2010).

my case study. I conducted interviews with the organizers, Sky and Hadar, two sex-positive activists with trans and non-binary experiences, and I participated in the workshop itself. The workshop was conceived of for trans, non-binary, and queer people who couldn't buy sex toys, and for those interested in making vegan sex toys. During the two-hour workshop, organizers showed simple techniques for turning recyclable materials (like some bicycle parts), plastic and silicone objects into whips, packers, harnesses and various body molds, and creative sex toys; participants then had time to experiment with the materials and create their own sex toys. In this chapter, I make particular reference to my interviews and my observations to identify and begin to theorize the specificity and critical potential of a trans-organizing modality of sexuality.

2   Conceptualizing a Trans-organizing Modality of Sexuality

The fact that sexuality is a production-apparatus of bodies and identities, built at the intersection of a multitude of socio-cultural discourses and practices, and involved in networks of control, negotiation, counter-production and resistance,[9] has been and continues to be widely studied in various fields, from sociology to feminist, women and gender studies. Recently, the organizational sciences have also developed an important, yet still marginalized, sub-discipline known as organizational sexuality,[10] which sees sexuality as a highly organized and organizing apparatus. This area of research has produced studies on the dynamics of power and the hetero-patriarchal norms that materialize in organizational and work spaces.[11] However, little research (if any) has taken into consideration organizations that promote a cultural shift in sexuality from a trans perspective.[12] These organizations, which are often collectives or activist-leaning nonprofits, are rarely taken seriously, either theoretically or empirically. The organizing processes in these contexts, which are volatile with respect to more formalized ones, are often considered disorganized, and thus irrelevant. My objective is to reappropriate the idea of *dis/organization* as a

---

9   Michel Foucault, *The History of Sexuality, Vol. 1,* (New York: Pantheon, 1978).

10   Jo Brewis, Melissa Tyler and Albert Mills, "Sexuality and Organizational Analysis – 30 Years On: Editorial Introduction," *Organization* 21, no. 3 (2014): 305–11.

11   The themes dealt with include exclusion/inclusion/capitalization of LG+ identities in the production of value, the specificities of sex work as a job, gender violence, and sexual harassment in the workplace.

12   Anshuman Prasad, Pushkala Prasad, Albert J. Mills, and Jean Helms Mills, *The Routledge Companion to Critical Management Studies,* (London: Routledge, 2016).

critical analytical tool and to show how, on the contrary, these organizations are a crucial point of reference for theorizing the organizing processes surrounding sexuality.

Trans experiences call into question, and thus critically interrogate, and dis/organize traditional ideas of sexuality, sex, and gender. Consequently, these organizations have the potential to propose alternative/innovative modes of thinking about and enacting, not just sexuality, but the very organizing processes around it as well. By putting three approaches in conversation, namely the study of social movements, trans studies, and theories of organizational practices, I propose conceptualizing the trans-organizing modality as a sector of social movement organizations. A social movement organization is a complex and dynamic organization affiliated with an oppositional movement that attempts to implement its objectives.[13] In this context, I recover the notion of *problematicity*,[14] which I define as the modalities with which discursive and material needs are articulated as problematic within an organization. What is problematized in a trans-organizing modality? What specific boundaries are redrawn?

Thinking of the trans-organizing modality as a problematizing social movement organization helps us understand its political dimension. This specifically has to do with *cis norms*, and the dynamics of power they create around organizing sexuality, sex and gender. Preciado has shown how the construction of sex is a cis-heterosocial technology.[15] This construction works by way of the fragmentation of the body, cutting up organs to transform them into the natural and anatomical center of gender difference (man/woman) a *heteropartitioning* of the body.[16] Some body parts (genitalia, for example) are thus abstracted and isolated, and become sexual and gender signifiers. These parts are then re-signified binarily in order to construct a "natural" subject (man/penis, woman/vagina) on the basis of a linear connection body-sex-gender.[17] Thus, on the one hand, the trans experience is subject to ideas like the naturalized body-sex-gender link, a normative link built as a line, and a binary, which this experience puts in crisis; on the other hand, this experience has the power

13   John D McCarthy, and Mayer N. Zald, "Resource Mobilization and Social movements: A Partial Theory," *American Journal of Sociology* 82, no. 6 (1997): 1212–41.

14   Aaron M. McCright and Riley E. Dunlap, "Challenging Global Warming as a Social Problem: An Analysis of the Conservative Movement's Counter-Claims," *Social Problems* 47, no. 4 (2000): 499–522.

15   Paul B Preciado, *Countersexual Manifesto*, (New York: Columbia University Press, 2018).

16   Ibid.

17   Judith Butler, *Gender Trouble: Feminism and the Subversion of Identity*, (New York: Routledge, 1990).

to make the body-sex-gender binarism visible as a dominant cis socio-cultural norm of control. Above all, the trans experience reveals the fact that this binary link body-sex-gender not only influences discourses on sexed subjects, but also those very organizing processes around sexuality. The cis norm is, in fact, at the foundation of the organizing onto-epistemologies, or rather, the *who/what* that the organizations know and recognize as existing, and the *how* they (don't) take them into account in their organizing processes.[18] The concurrence of a tendency toward the heteronormativized genitalization of desire and sexuality, and the pathologization of trans experience on the basis of a (cis)genderization of genitalia, reinforces cis-normative epistemologies and creates barriers in the production of knowledge about sexuality from a trans perspective. A trans-organizing modality could navigate through, and oppose, this dominant epistemology, and counter-produce knowledge. I would like to speculate that a trans-organizing modality of sexuality counter-produces, not only through the production of new ideas, but also through what Nicolini and Gherardi call *practices*: materially mediated "doing" and "saying."[19] To be precise, I am referring to "doing" and "saying" as *formative practices*. Gherardi and Perrotta define *formativity* as the type of knowledge generated in the process of creating the *object* of the practice, and that gets expressed while the *object* in question takes shape.[20] What kind of practices generate and express themselves in the process of creating an *object* through a trans perspective? The theoretical frame that I have just mapped out allows us to concentrate our analysis of these practices in this context.

3   The Do-It-Yourself Workshop and Its Dis/Organizing Dynamics

Three dis-organizing foci emerge from the analysis of the gathered material, centering on the body, on language, and on the sharing of sexual knowledge.

---

18   Ludovico Virtù, "A Self-Reflexive Approach to Trans Embodiment in the Context of the Sex Toy Industry," (Paper Presented at Cirque, Centro interuniversitario di recerca queer, conference, Aquila, March 30-April 2 2017).

19   Silvia Gherardi and Davide Nicolini, "Il pensiero pratico. Un'etnografia dell'apprendimento," *Rassegna italiana di sociologia* 42, no. 2 (2001): 231–56.

20   Silvia Gherardi and Manuela Perrotta, "Between the Hand and the Head: How Things Get Done, and How in Doing the Ways of Doing are Discovered," *Qualitative Research in Organizations and Management: An International Journal* 9, no. 2 (2014): 134–50.

3.1   Dis/Organizing the Body

Sky, an activist involved in organizing the do-it-yourself sex toy workshop, notices a lack of attention to trans and non-binary communities in the production and circulation of sex toys: "I noticed that trans people usually don't have access to sex toys that reflect their needs." Sky observes how trans people often don't have access to sex toys that adapt to the diversities and varieties of their bodies: "The toys in circulation are adaptable to trans people that are not transitioning[21] or are made based on one sole idea of how transitioning trans people are." This lack of attention is tied to the absence of an imaginary of trans bodies in a cis and transnormative epistemology (how are/must trans bodies be?). As Sky maintains: "In reality many people's bodies are *in-between*," stressing a spectrum of diversity in the corporeality of trans and non-binary people. In particular, these corporealities dismantle the binarism of the linear body-sex-gender link, rendering visible the idea that the parts/technologies of the body that are constructed as "sex" are various and modifiable, just like the pleasures tied to them. For example, referring to the technologies of the body that often, but aren't always part of a desired transition, Sky declares: "There is no sex toy for trans men with a metoidioplasty[22] and rarely are sex toys geared toward the functions and sensitivity specific to a phalloplasty."[23] Some transitions have a material impact on bodies, on morphologies, and on the pleasures of trans people, but very little is said about this. In this way the workshop becomes a space in which it is possible to openly discuss stigmatized technologies and unknown pleasures. For example, because of new hormones or because of surgeries like metoidioplasty or phalloplasty, the bodies of trans men and trans masculine people develop and acquire specific functions and sensitivities. "If you learn to make your own sex toys, you can adapt them to whatever body you have," says Sky, enthusiastically. Do-it-yourself makes it possible for trans people to examine and turn to these specificities, and becomes a potential way

---

21   For non-transitioning I am referring to trans people who choose not to take hormones and/or not undergo medical-surgical interventions, or those who do not have access to them. Not all trans people use this term to describe their experiences. In this space I have decided to respect the language used by the people being interviewed.

22   Genital reconstruction surgery which entails vaginal closure, the reconstruction of the urethra and the reconstruction of a genital morphology generally called a penis through the use of the genital morphology generally called a clitoris. The nerves of the original genital morphology are thus the same in the reconstructed morphology.

23   Genital reconstruction surgery which entails the reconstruction of a genital morphology generally called a penis, through the use of tissue taken from other parts of the body. The nerves of the genital morphology generally called a clitoris are transferred to the reconstructed morphology.

of recognizing the diversities of trans bodies, the spectrum of trans embodiment. Thus, it is a formative practice, a way (mediated, but not immediate) to
know and recognize alternative embodiment. As Sky maintains: "I still don't
have all the answers, but I am trying to push trans people to be inventive and
to make sex toys that are suited to non-ordinary bodies, even if in reality it
is hard for me as well." Do-it-yourself is a journey of becoming, in which the
epistemological linearity between an already known body, and the production
of objects that reflect the needs of such a body, is broken in order to create
new knowledges (about body and pleasure) that emerge precisely through this
do-it-yourself practice: making your own sex toys so that your trans body isn't
un/known, but also re/discovering the sensitivities of your own body through
do-it-yourself production.

3.2 Dis/Organizing Language

The activists with whom I spoke are very attentive to questions of language
within organizing processes. As you can read in the opening text on the flyer
for the event in question, they call for a reflection on the limits of identity
categories: "When we try to assign clear categories to people so much gets lost.
Between men and women, straight and gay, sexual and asexual, between all
these categories there is space, space for, well, all the rest." The imposition of
fixed and "obvious" categories limits the meanings and experiences tied to
gender, sexual orientation, asexuality, because in reality many experiences
(whether they are tied to such categories or excluded by them) are developed
in a spectrum. Between categorical identity binarisms there is space for a
gamut of experiences (trans, transgender, mtf, ftm, intersex, kinky, etc.). These
activists, as you can read in the description, propose creating and exploring
this space of imaginaries and experiences, precisely through the organization
of their event: "To explore that space, to name, and deconstruct those same
names, and in particular to celebrate that space." And thus language once
more becomes central: the creation of a new alternative language (that gives
new names to bodies and experiences), but at the same time the deconstruction, the constant calling into question of this language. Language becomes a
powerful yet volatile practice, a volatility that is not disorganized, but rather
it is the dis/organization needed for the fluidity, complexity and contextual-
ization of identities and experiences, in particular those that are trans, non-
binary, and queer. Dis/organizing language thus becomes a formative interactive practice that is enacted when one relates to their own experience and to
the experience of others.

This practice happens even in the process of making do-it-yourself sex
toys. In reference to the organization of the workshop, Sky notes: "I will never

say: this is an object for trans men or this is an object for trans women, or this is an object for people with a penis. But, for example, this object is like this and it could be suitable for some bodies and not for others. I try not to impose a gender on sex toys, and instead, I specifically try to de-gender objects and practices that are usually associated with gender." This practice of de-gendering, tied to the do-it-yourself action, is imposed on the objects, but it is a mediated operation that does not want to take the embodiments or identities of those involved for granted. As Sky explains: "I am trying to de-gender sex and sex toys, there is no reason to assign gender them unless you want to, unless that's sexy for you." This formative practice allows possibilities to emerge for trans and non-binary people in particular, to live and share the spectrum of their embodiments and identifications through an often erratic and contextualized re-gendering that emerges from desire.

3.3   Dis/Organizing the Sharing of Sexual Knowledge

In the experience of the activists I spoke with, there is a recurrent reflection on the processes of sharing knowledge that is both personal and organizational. As Hadar explains: "We don't know something and think *oh wow* things are hard to do. But you know what? Seriously a lot depends on the patriarchy." There is a strong awareness that these processes are influenced by normative power structures, and thus do-it-yourself becomes a political practice of empowerment, even in the conceptualization of d-i-y sex toys. "You know, when you're little, you believe in these things: I can't do this, I'm not stable enough, I'm not focused enough, I can't do it. And then you discover that it's not true. You need to practice, destroy a few of your models, but you can learn to do practically anything," Hadar says. The theme of the do-it-yourself learning processes returns in the way in which these activists think of the organization of the workshop, which develops through the lens of collective learning. As Sky explains: "My intention is to say: look I'm not perfect, I read the *funzines*, I tried some things and, let's take them as a jumping off point for the workshop, not so much through a teacher-student dynamic, but through a collective learning dynamic." Just as many social movements refuse learning hierarchies, these activists are more concerned with not assuming positions of authority, than with exposing themselves to potential stigmatization because of their trans, non-binary, non-normative experiences. As Sky confesses: "I'm not scared of talking about my sex life, I am more scared of being seen as an authority on the subject because I am in no way an expert. So I will try to make clear that I am still learning, that we are all here to learn, and so we will try to collaborate. I hope that people sense this and aren't disappointed when I don't have all the answers." The research and implementation of this alternative learning methodology is a work in progress that is tied to the desire to create a reparative, safe space for those involved. As Sky explains: "There are various approaches to creating a safe space. My most common approach is personal vulnerability, I mean if I speak openly about my sex life and my situation, usually the space gets created." This alternative learning methodology is particularly activated by trans experience. Sky continues: "I feel fairly at ease speaking of some things that other people experience as a source of vulnerability, for example, transitioning and talking about being trans to cis people. Often people live this experience with extreme vulnerability, so if I come out as a trans person and talk about my transition, this helps them talk about things that they live through with vulnerability. In some way I learned to use it as a social technique, to create a space for shame and vulnerability and insecurity, trying to be the most vulnerable person in the space." Here the trans experience itself becomes a tool, and vulnerability is the method that makes alternative learning processes possible. "People are used to authoritarian environments in which a person possesses all the knowledge, but I love workshops that are not hierarchical and are instead based on sharing, and collective learning," Sky concluded.

4 Trans-organizing, Sexuality and Formative Practices

At the beginning of this chapter I asked myself what might characterize a trans-organizing modality of sexuality. I conceptualized the trans-organizational mode around sexuality as a complex and dynamic organization that opposes a cis-heteronormative culture, and tries to implement an alternative production through formative practices. In the specific case of the trans perspective do-it-yourself sex toy workshop, a trans-organizing modality calls into question the traditional ideas of sexuality through the same organizing processes, or rather dis/organizes sexuality through practices that problematize cis-normative ideas of embodiment, language, and shared sexual knowledge, which simultaneously creates an alternative epistemology of sexuality. Having said that, what are the experiential challenges that trans and non-binary people deal with in regard to this? What political challenges are there in our research and our movements? In other words, what could a reflection on a trans-organizing modality of sexuality mean?

As a trans activist and researcher, I want to conclude with a theoretical-political reflection on the intersection of trans and sexuality. Examining a trans-organizing modality of sexuality leads us to reflect, first and foremost, on the socio-cultural obstacles that trans and non-binary people face with regard to sexuality, including the invisibility and stigmatization of their embodiments and pleasure, the imposition of a cis-normative binary vision of bodies and identities, and the difficulty of finding safe spaces. This stigmatization feeds a lack of awareness and shared knowledge: little is known, for example, about the complex relationships between identity, morphological changes and pleasures from a trans perspective, and few studies are interested in the intersection between trans and sexuality from theoretical, empirical, and experiential perspectives. Even within trans movements there is reticence about speaking openly about people's own bodies, doubts, and pleasures in relation to morphologies, sexual practices, and desires, despite the existence of an interesting counter-production of grassroots erotic imaginaries that go from the organizing of workshops to alternative porn production. Yet, organizing practices that allow for the counter-production of knowledge and alternative modes of organizing sexuality from a trans perspective exist, and they can help us rethink our conceptions of sexuality in a way that is more inclusive of trans and non-binary experiences. This involves, first and foremost, moving beyond (in our ways of thinking and our interpretive frameworks) the idea that only two standard bodies that are easily identifiable exist, so that we may recognize a spectrum of diversity in embodiment, sensitivities, and pleasures. Simultaneously, we must change our language when we interact with others, and enact a de-gendering and re-gendering of sexuality, and the sexes, to include this spectrum of bodily and identity diversity. This journey is not easy, and it cannot just be a rhetorical stratagem ("whoever is welcome," "sexuality is for all"), it must be a journey, taken on and shared by all, that is enacted to rethink the way in which organizing is done, the material and linguistic processes that organizing entails, and those who are called upon to organize. What collaborations happen between trans and cis people? Who is exposed and how? Who makes their own vulnerabilities into a method, and what does this suggest for the ways in which organizing power circulates? What kind of imaginaries are produced and shared, and how? A trans-organizing modality pushes us to use alternative methodologies of knowledge sharing that often include high affective intensity, vulnerability, personal exposure, and the risk of stigmatization, but that have the experiential and political power to make new forms of knowledge and interrelation emerge.[24] I believe that it is necessary not only to include trans and non-binary people in decisive organizational processes, but also to give value to trans and non-binary knowledges and methods. By

---

24   Nat Raha, "Transfeminine Brokenness, Radical Transfeminism," *South Atlantic Quarterly* 116, no. 3 (2017): 632–46; Mijke Van der Drift, "Radical Romanticism, Violent Cuteness, and the Destruction of the World," *Journal of Aesthetics & Culture* 10, no. 2 (2018).

collaborating on the creation of safe spaces that centralize trans and non-binary voices, an alternative epistemology of sexuality emerges that takes into account trans and non-binary experiences in a process that affects everyone. This operation, however, can't just be rhetorical, it must constantly interrogate spaces, practices and their organization through a political lens.[25] The organization of sexuality must be studied and implemented as a series of affective and material discursive practices that pay attention to the epistemologies and contextualized powers that influence and shape the borders of the imaginaries and spaces of sexualities: who has a position of organizing power, how is this power circulated and shared, and who is excluded/included/rendered invisible/removed, how can we "do" and "speak" sexuality differently?

Works Cited

Brewis, Jo, Melissa Tyler and Albert Mills. "Sexuality and Organizational Analysis – 30 Years On: Editorial Introduction." *Organization* 21, no. 3 (2014): 305–11.

Butler, Judith. *Gender Trouble: Feminism and the Subversion of Identity*. New York: Routledge, 1990.

Foucault, Michel. *The History of Sexuality, Vol. 1*. New York: Pantheon, 1978.

Gherardi, Silvia and Davide Nicolini. "Il pensiero pratico. Un'etnografia dell'apprendimento." *Rassegna italiana di sociologia* 42, no. 2 (2001): 231–56.

Gherardi, Silvia and Manuela Perrotta. "Between the Hand and the Head: How Things Get Done, and How in Doing the Ways of Doing are Discovered." *Qualitative Research in Organizations and Management: An International Journal* 9, no. 2 (2014): 134–50.

Kondelin, Sade. "Dis/Orientations of Gender and Sexuality in Transgender Embodiment." SQS-*Suomen Queer-tutkimuksen Seuran lehti* 8, no. 1–2 (2014): 32–43.

McCarthy, John D. and Mayer N. Zald. "Resource Mobilization and Social movements: A Partial Theory." *American Journal of Sociology* 82, no. 6 (1997): 1212–41.

McCright, Aaron M. and Riley E. Dunlap. "Challenging Global Warming as a Social Problem: An Analysis of the Conservative Movement's Counter-Claims." *Social Problems* 47, no. 4 (2000): 499–522.

Pignedoli, Clark. "Beyond Trans Medicalization: Gatekeeping and the Epistemological Privilege of Ignorance." Paper presented at Cirque (Centro interuniversitario di recerca queer): L'Aquila, 2017.

---

25   Mijke Van der Drift, Hunter Chryssy, and Raha Nat, "Radical Transfeminism: The End Times of a Failed Political Myth," panel presented at Trans*Studies Conference, (University of Arizona: Tucson, 2016).

Prasad, Anshuman, Pushkala Prasad, Albert J. Mills, and Jean Helms Mills. *The Routledge Companion to Critical Management Studies.* London: Routledge, 2016.

Preciado, Paul (Beatriz). *Countersexual Manifesto.* New York: Columbia University Press, 2018.

Raha, Nat. "Transfeminine Brokenness, Radical Transfeminism." *South Atlantic Quarterly* 116, no. 3 (2017): 632–46.

Salamon, Gayle. *Assuming a Body: Transgender and Rhetorics of Materiality.* New York: Columbia University Press, 2010.

Serano, Julia. *Whipping Girl: A Transsexual Woman on Sexism and the Scapegoating of Femininity.* Berkeley: Seal Press, 2007.

Stryker, Susan. *Transgender History: The Roots of Today's Revolution.* Berkeley: Seal Press, 2008.

Van der Drift, Mijke. "Radical Romanticism, Violent Cuteness, and the Destruction of the World." *Journal of Aesthetics & Culture* 10, no. 2 (2018).

Virtù, Ludovico. "A Self-Reflexive Approach to Trans Embodiment in the Context of the Sex Toy Industry." Paper presented at the Cirque, Centro interuniversitario di recerca queer conference: L'Aquila, 2017.

Virtù, Ludovico "Displacing the Gender Binary Through Modes of Dis/organizing: Sex Toys, Sexuality and Trans Politics." *Politics and Governance,* 8, no.3 (2020): 321–331.

CHAPTER 4

Virtual Interfaces of Biotech Reproduction

Angela Balzano

We live in the era of bio-info-potentiality; technological mediation is so imma-
nent in all our lives that it has become impossible to discern the borders
between nature and technology, desire and necessity. It is less and less logical
to think of material reality as representing the polar opposite of virtual reality.
We live in an era of augmented reality and we invest more and more in medical-
pharmaceutical research: thanks to this, the average human life expectancy
in the so-called Western World has increased by about twenty-three years in
little more than a century. However, this prolonged lifespan affects countries
that are experiencing a simultaneous decrease in population and postponed
reproduction. Let's consider the data from the Eurostat Regional Yearbook
2015: European women continue to reproduce less frequently and later in life.
The average age of women at the time of their first pregnancy went from 29.0
to 30.4 between 2001 and 2014. In 2015 the birth rate in Europe was 1.58. For a
more concrete idea of this population decrease let's compare the birth rate in
2015, 5 million, to those in 1964, 7.7 million. For context, let's remember that
in countries with the highest GDP, the standard is 2.1 live births per woman.[1]
Technologies of life make themselves felt in this scenario. In light of this data,
it may not seem coincidental that more assisted fertility attempts are carried
out in Europe than any other part of the world.[2]

Reproductive medicine is developed in the context of a bio-info-mediated
society. Biotechnologies would not be so complex without the cyber-info-
technological component, but without the information sciences and the communication devices they wouldn't be so familiar either. Information about
techniques of assisted fertility travels over the web, on patient blogs, homepages of private clinics, social networks and private chats. This contribution
moves in a zig-zag across the webpages of gamete agencies and clinics for

---

1 European Statistics Office. "Statistics Explained." Eurostat Statistics Explained. https://ec.eur
   opa.eu/eurostat/statistics-explained/index.php?title=Fertility_statistics.
2 European IVF-Monitoring Consortium (EIM) for the European Society of Human
   Reproduction and Embryology (ESHRE), "Assisted Reproductive Technology in Europe, 2012.
   Results Generated from European Registers by ESHRE," in *Human Reproduction*, 31(8), 2016:
   1638–52.

assisted fertility cycles. The goal is to understand which narratives and representations make headway, which virtual imaginary underlies the promise of assured reproduction.

Let's geolocalize the analysis. We are in Italy, in 2017, looking for a way to bring a third-party gamete pregnancy to term. Quite likely, we will be guided by the normative geo-political-economic context to consult internet sites and blogs searching for an effective solution, which may be abroad. If we recall that until 2014 the use of foreign gametes by intentional parents was prohibited by the law 40/2004, then we will also understand that until that same year Italian residents unfailingly followed this path: different trips on and offline between clinics and gamete agencies. With the ruling 164/2015, the Supreme Court tried to rebalance the burdens caused by the Catholic fundamentalism intrinsic to law 40, declaring Articles 4, 9, and 12 unconstitutional, and abolishing the codes that prohibited recourse to foreign gamete donors in the case of absolute infertility. In 2014, the Conference of regions and autonomous provinces presented the government with guidelines that included the "rule for free and voluntary donation of reproductive cells."[3] People who donate gametes would not receive any financial compensation, but would "eventually be paid for any missed days of work."[4] In 2015 the Minister of Health responded in support of the regions.[5] The availability of gametes, particularly oocytes, is insufficient in Italy. Elisabetta Coccia, head of the CECOS Scientific Centers for Fertility, explained that "donation of oocyte on behalf of women who are doing homologous fertility, or egg-sharing, is not sufficient, and Italy has not seen many voluntary donations as of this moment. The choice to make arrangements abroad remains the only viable path to guarantee heterologous fecundation in our country."[6]

If we consider waiting times at public clinics, then the reasons for seeking out a foreign clinic online increase. In Sicily the wait is nearly eighteen months, fifteen in Veneto and twelve in Liguria.[7] Donation being the only means to procure gametes has not made things better. Private centers connected to foreign clinics multiply, and can be contacted via online platforms. If we type

---

3   Conference of Regions and Autonomous Provinces, 14/109/CRO2/ C7SAN, 2.
4   Ibid., 13.
5   DM n. 161, July 1st, 2015 viewable at: *Istituto superiore di sanità*, www.iss.it.
6   Ibid. Translation is our own.
7   "Fecondazione, liste attesa centri pubblici: da 18 mesi Sicilia a zero Toscana," *Adnkronos*, Oct. 6, 2015, www.adnkronos.com/salute/sanita/2015/10/06/fecondazione-liste-attesa-centri-pub blici-mesi-sicilia-toscana_grH2JivQtPA61VW1OHAwCK.html?refresh_ce.

"assisted heterologous fecundation,"[8] the second result Google offers[9] is the Eugin Clinic,[10] and the page is "In Vitro Fertilization with Donor Ova and the Partner's Sperm." The Eugin Clinic defines heterologous fertilization thusly: "a laboratory technique wherein a donor's eggs are fertilized with your partner's sperm." This definition is as telling as it is mystifying, right from the moment it only defines in vitro insemination that involves oocyte from a third woman as heterologous, excluding the possibility that intentional parents could be seeking a male gamete. The spermatozoa could come from a donor, or the ovum could have been cryo-frozen from the same patient: it would still be FIVET (Fertilization in Vitro and Embryo Transfer). After this first erroneous definition, further explanation of the scientific process is offered; the site moves on to reassure the potential patient about the liabilities and ethics of Spanish civil codes. A pink square appears next to the main text: "pre-diagnosis online;" by clicking, one can enter in ones' information. The first prompt the Eugin Clinic offers includes options that, to this day, are forbidden by law 40: "I want to be a mother ... a) with my male partner; b) on my own; c) with my female partner."[11] Considering Article 5 of law 40 that prohibits the recourse to technology by people who aren't coupled, and by LGBTQ people, when faced with options b and c, the Clinic explains that: "In Italy, assisted fertility treatment is not permitted for single women or women with female partners. In Spain, however, Spanish law allows all women to access treatment for assisted fertility, regardless of civil status or sexual orientation. An Italian team carries out these treatments in Barcelona." If, on the other hand, we choose the option "I want to be a mother with my male partner," we are asked our age and to indicate any possible problems either partner may have. Based on the information given, the page will redirect us to the results of the online pre-diagnosis. If we indicate a problem of insufficiency of oocyte in the woman, and a low-quality spermatozoa

---

8   The expression "heterologous fecundation" is scientifically wrong, the Google results were imposed on these keywords because of their widespread usage, but it is useful to recall that "from the scientific point of view, the term *heterologous* indicates the encounter between gametes of different species" [Carlo Flamigni and Andrea Borini, *Fecondazione and e(s)terologa,* (Rome: L'asino d'oro edizioni, 2012), p.49].

9   The first result is an article from 2015 titled "Heterologous Fecundation, What is it and Who Can do it?" [Valentina Arcovio, "Fecondazione eterologa, cos'è e chi la può fare?" *Il secolo XIX,* March 10, 2015, https://www.ilsecoloxix.it/salute-benessere/2015/03/10/news/fecondazione-eterologa-cos-e-e-chi-la-puo-fare-1.31663283.

10   "In Vitro Fertilization with Donor Ova and the Partner's Sperm," *Eugin Clinic,* www.eugin.it/trattamenti/fecondazione-eterologa.

11   "Pre-Diagnosis Online," *Eugin Clinic,* https://www.eugin.it/riproduzione-assistita-pre-diagnosi-online.

in the man, the suggested therapy is FIVET with "donor oocyte and the partner's sperm." In truth, patients should be reminded that in the case of low-quality spermatozoa, other therapies may be necessary for the man as well, but the clinic chooses to focus exclusively on the harvesting of oocytes. The underlying argument is an interesting one, if nature tries to force us to reproduce before a certain age, technology allows us to work around it: "the ova lose their reproductive capacity in an irreversible process that intensifies after the age of 35. This biological reality was, years ago, the end of the path towards maternity. Today, innovations in the technology of assisted fertility allow us to keep the dream of motherhood alive; we help thousands of women from all over the world overcome the difficulties imposed by nature."[12]

Nature is not venerated here, nor is it dialectically opposed to technology, rather, it is sexualized and reinvented. Not one question has been asked about our sex since the beginning of our online pre-diagnosis. The clinic has taken for granted that it is a woman submitting herself to the pre-diagnosis, speaking only about maternity and never about parenthood, choosing pink as the dominant color. The possibility of a man seeking information online is excluded. Maternity is the focus; the communication strategy of so many fertility clinics is to leverage this desire for maternity, to take aim at a precise target. Think of the declaration of the gynecological director of the Valencian Institute for Infertility (IVI): "there are more and more women who decide to become mothers after the age of 40 [...] Women over 40 with independent, stable careers: this is the profile of the patients that make this type of choice."[13]

In comparison to the homepage of the Eugin Clinic, that features the face of a white-blond-blue-eyed woman, the homepage of IVI focuses more explicitly on the "dream of maternity," making use of a promising, reassuring virtual fantasy. Here the image features a woman and newborn (both white), that embrace and look at one another. The banner with images and links alternates a picture of a faceless pregnant woman, and a close-up of a peaceful smiling woman. The picture of the belly is associated with the link "Guaranteed Pregnancy," that catapults us onto a soft couch where a woman is lying down, comfortably cuddling a baby in her arms.[14]

The communication strategy is direct and ironic. The picture instills security, the couch and the embraced baby form a ready-made family, but the accompanying text hints at the difficulties of maternity: "Many women dream of being

---

12   Ibid.
13   "Frequently Asked Questions," *IVI*, https://ivitalia.it/domande-frequenti/donne-single/.
14   https://ivitalia.it/garanzia-gravidanza.

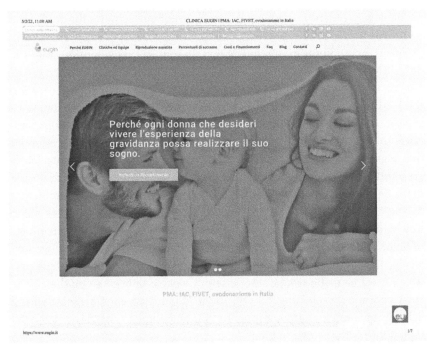

FIGURE 4.1 Assisted reproduction website

FIGURE 4.2 Website mission statement: Your dream of being a mother is our duty

mothers even though they know what a pregnancy consists of: sleeping poorly, gaining weight, crying for no reason, being tired all the time.

This is why, if your dream to be a mother is so great, at IVI we work with patients in the program for assisted in vitro fertility with donor eggs (donation of oocytes), guaranteeing pregnancy in a maximum of three cycles. If you do not achieve pregnancy, patients will receive reimbursement for the cost of the treatment."

This is a communication strategy that aims at shifting attention from the difficulties of the cycles of IVF, to those of every maternity. Despite the promissory nature of the object of sale, the clinic offers a certainty from the outset, the kind of certainty typical of the "satisfaction or refund" liberal apparatus transposed onto a post-Fordist production system. The clinic works to "produce" a maximum of three attempts, the patient/client may request a refund if the pregnancy, the good of production, is not obtained. All psychological labels are omitted, the language is that of a typical financial transaction. No allusion to the delusion that could follow not achieving pregnancy, the only problem is related to the financial investment, not to the emotional-affective investment. Nowhere on the pages we visited is there information about the percentage of failures, not even on the page "Heterogenous Fecundation." Here, we find a video that explains: "The donation of oocytes makes the miracle of life possible for women who would otherwise not be able to become mothers." The video continues, explaining that the oocyte "donors" are carefully selected and "a highly qualitative computer program combines human criteria to match the right donor with the right patient."[15]

Despite being a high-tech clinic, it presents IVF as a provider of the "miracle of life." Fragmented nature is thus recomposed, maternity is re-naturalized, and genders are reconfirmed. It will always be a woman who brings the pregnancy to term, it does not matter if the couple is heterosexual or not, and the moment of birth will always be a miracle. This is the message promoted on the pages we visited; a message that attempts to veil in nostalgia that which we are currently living. In fact, as Rosi Braidotti claims, today we must recognize that "the maternal function and hence the reproduction of the human in its bio-cultural mode has become simultaneously disengaged from the female body [...] It has also, however, been re-naturalized."[16] Braidotti's analysis effectively describes the current dual tendency – so explicitly stated in the homepages we visited – to reinsert the "female maternal" into a reinvented natural order, while at the same time inscribing it in the techno-industrial market of assisted fertilization.

In this way, the rhetoric of the sacredness of reproduction resurfaces, even in the era of the intersection between technological apparatuses and bio-tech markets; but, as it surpasses nature in the name of the miracle of life, insisting

15   "Donating eggs in IVI–Donation of Ova or Oocytes in Spain," *IVI Italia*, youtube video, July
        8, 2013. www.youtube.com/watch?v=tzfzzmgZ9ws.
16   Rosi Braidotti, *Transpositions: On Nomadic Ethics* (Polity Press: Cambridge UK, 2006), 49.

exclusively on the "dream of motherhood," isn't it using new tools to re-present us with the old existential recipe of wife-mother?

As Simone de Beauvoir already brilliantly explained: One is not born, but rather becomes, a woman, and it could be that not all those who become women also want to be mothers.[17] It could be that a homosexual man has a stronger desire to form a family than a heterosexual woman does, and that today the new technologies of life reveal themselves to be very useful in satisfying his desire for parenthood. The "offerings" of the clinics studied seem limiting, not to mention contradictory, at a time when the technologies of reproductive medicine could permit the exchange of genders and roles, sex changes and the personalization of sexuality and parenthood. Doesn't affirming that assisted reproduction technologies make the "miracle of life" possible mean adding something akin to religious faith to technoscience?

Science has always had a difficult relationship with religion, this is evident in the efforts to universalize science by searching for a single law/force to explain the complexities of life: the god-force. As Deleuze and Guattari argue in *What is Philosophy?*, such an outcome is not possible, not because such a law does not exist, but because in order to follow this research to its conclusion, science would have to abandon its frame of reference, and instead adopt a frame of transcendence, which is typical of religion.[18] This does not, however, exclude the possibility of implementing these same apparatuses of pastoral power within a mutated socio-economic and geopolitical context; or, of using the same rhetorical armory, and the same Western-Christian imaginary to present the latest scientific developments on sexuality and reproduction in a less morally controversial manner. From this, albeit quick and partial, panorama of the main Italian-language fertility clinic sites, we learned the following: the deployed imaginary is drenched in mystery and sacredness, openly contradicting the reality in which assisted reproductive technologies are developed and spread. In fact, life science and information science are not emancipated from divine will, doctors are not saints and scientists are not god. Human life is by no means a miracle, but a relatively recent historic-politico-technological invention. Restrictive laws and regulations centered on heterosexuality, marketing and communications strategies drenched in whiteness, and publicity campaigns saturated in maternal essentialism, would like to silence the subversive potential of the new life technologies. The mutations underway, however, are multiple and viral, subjective and collective, virtual and material: for

---

17   Simone De Beauvoir, *The Second Sex* (New York: Vintage Books, 1973).

18   Giles Deleuze and Felix Guattari, *What is Philosophy?*, (New York: Columbia University Press, 1996).

many, sexuality and reproduction are territories explored beyond the confines of pre-established sexes and genders.

Works Cited

Adnkronos. "Fecondazione, liste attesa centri pubblici: da 18 mesi Sicilia a zero Toscana." Oct. 6, 2015. www.adnkronos.com/salute/sanita/2015/10/06/fecondazi one-liste-attesa-centri-pubblici-mesi-sicilia-toscana_grH2JivQtPA61VW1OHAwCK .html?refresh_ce.

Braidotti, Rosi. *Transpositions: On Nomadic Ethics.* Cambridge UK: Polity Press, 2006.

Deleuze, Giles and Felix Guattari. *What is Philosophy?* New York: Columbia University Press, 1996.

European IVF-monitoring Consortium (EIM), European Society of Human Reproduction and Embryology (ESHRE), C Calhaz-Jorge, C de Geyter, M S Kupka, J de Mouzon, K Erb, et al. "Assisted Reproductive Technology in Europe, 2012: Results Generated from European Registers by ESHRE." *Human Reproduction* 31, no. 8 (2016): 1638–52. https://doi.org/10.1093/humrep/dew151.

Flamigni, Carlo and Andrea Borini. *Fecondazione and e(s)terologa.* Rome: L'asino d'oro edizioni, 2012.

CHAPTER 5

Objection Denied

Obiezione Respinta

The virtual space of the web 2.0 is an environment that is constantly traversed by acts of violence toward migrants, women, and subjects who don't conform to the heterosexual norm.[1] Everyday there are episodes of slut shaming, cyber-bullying, and discrimination that are, nevertheless, ignored in stories by mass-media. These same media that indulge toxic stories about male violence against women—women who are depicted as the victims of "too much love"–ignore how this violence operates in virtual environments, and is normalized by policies of the most globally popular social networks. Even Facebook, which tries to get rid of images of women's nipples, or menstruation stains, never takes a strong position against the violence that women are subjected to within this social network.[2]

This fact doesn't surprise us: "digital technologies are not separable from the material realities that underwrite them"[3] and, in fact, on Facebook the patriarchal power structure of the reality in which we live is reproduced. On the web we witness the normalization of these same group practices and dynamics that we see on the streets or in the establishments we frequent. Similarly, the justification of rape on the basis of presumed behaviors, or the provocative clothing of the woman who was raped, is not different from the mechanisms that legitimize the sharing of hardcore videos or photos secretly obtained and exchanged on Facebook or WhatsApp. Where there's no consent there's violence, even in the digital realm. Only recently has Facebook made small steps forward when it comes to privacy and security to combat this kind of phenomenon, but it is still insufficient. We must respond to this cyber-bullying, this discrimination, and these web violences with a cyberfeminism that is careful to

---

1   This piece was penned by a group called "Obiezione Respinta." We are choosing to translate this as "Objection Denied" because it is evocative of the legal arena in which this conversation takes place, but it has previously been referred to as "Objection Rejected."

2   Eretica, among others, has publicly denounced them: "Facebook is only interested in erasing female nipples, menstruation stains, and expressions of body self-determination, but has nothing to say about the thousands of insults these women receive." Eretica Precari(A), "Facebook, pubblicare foto di donne senza consenso è uno stupor," (blog) *Il fatto quotidiano*, Jan 18th, 2017. ilfattoquotidiano.it.

3   Laboria Cubonix and Helen Hester, *The Xenofeminist Manifesto*, (New York: Verso, 2018), 8.

identify the critical points on the web, re-elaborating the way of being online, through a series of actions that reinvent the virtual space, to make it inclusive and safe, and accessible to all the queer and non-heteronormative singularities.

Our point of departure was the "Non una di meno" global feminist network that, in the last few years, has invaded public squares all over the world. Women have begun speaking in first person about their life conditions, overturning the dominant discourse that sees women as merely victims to protect, as objects and never subjects of the action. Speaking up, getting out of isolation, building a network: these are the conflicting and collective responses that we have identified to break free from male violence. This was our point of departure when thinking of one of the many levels on which gender violence operates, that devious and petty violence which is also present in public institutions like hospitals, pharmacies and medical aid offices: conscientious objection.

In Italy, though formally guaranteed under law 194, the right to terminate a pregnancy is often denied. Conscientious objection has reached a worrying level: the percentage of medical objectors on a national level is 70.7% with peaks that go well beyond 80% in some regions, while 40% of Italian hospitals do not offer services to voluntarily terminate pregnancy.[4] The social stigma and guilt for those women that choose to abort are still very strong, and heavy administrative sanctions are imposed on those who are forced to abort clandestinely,[5] a practice to which they turn precisely because of the difficulty in finding hospital assistance. Furthermore, even access to contraception is often hindered by the insufficient number of active clinics in town centers, and by the presence of pharmacists that refuse to sell contraceptives, as they practice conscientious objection that is explicitly prohibited by law but tolerated in practice.[6]

We are talking about a violence that is so widespread and systemic that, within our collective, we have found ourselves sharing our experiences of

---

4   Governmental report on the carrying out of law 194/78 – final data 2014 and 2015.

5   Clandestine abortion was, in fact, recently decriminalized, but monetary sanctions were drastically increased. Legislative decree January 15, 2016, n. 8 "Regulations for decriminalization, according to the norms of article 2, comma 2 of the April 28, 2014 law n. 67."

6   The Court of Gorizia, with its December 15, 2016 sentence, in fact, absolved the pharmacist who was accused of negligence: though working for the government run pharmacy, and thus employed by the public sector. During a night shift six years ago, she refused to deliver the drug Norlevo, claiming conscientious objection despite being shown a medical prescription that expressly indicated the drug had to be taken that same day. Rosella Gemma, "Pillola del giorno dopo, Tribunale di Gorizia assolve farmacista obiettrice," *Farmacista33*, December 20, 2016, http://www.farmacista33.it/pillola-del-giorno-dopo-tribunale-di-gorizia-assolve-farmacista-obiettrice/politica-e-sanita/news--38435.html?word=gorizia.

violence to which we were subject because we were women, workers, precarious laborers, and students looking for services that should have been guaranteed but instead are denied. One of our initial priorities was to get out of our local "bubble," putting our experiences on the web on a national level, to create a map of the hospital and pharmaceutical structures, general practitioners, clinics, objectors and not. A map that didn't stem from the data from the ministry of health: official data that most certainly cannot be considered neutral, that do not take into account the actual conditions of Italian health establishments, nor of the enormous difficulties women face in accessing pregnancy termination services.[7]

The model we were inspired by is a bottom-up inquiry model, or rather, one based on our daily experiences. In a few words, an inquiry that starts from us, and that isn't satisfied with official data that celebrates the decline of abortions nationally[8] but does not interrogate the actual wellness conditions of half of the national population.

Starting from the city of Pisa, where we are, we developed a map that can be accessed at obiezionerespinta.info. All of the information was gathered thanks to the reporting and accounts of women throughout Italy. The different structures (hospitals, pharmacies, clinics, general practitioners, anti-violence centers, and queer counseling services) are distinguished by the different "pins;" each pin is assigned a color, green or red, based on whether the report is positive or negative, and purple to mark the anti-violence centers and queer counselors. Clicking on a pin you can get information about the hours of operation, the phone numbers, and you can read testimonials given by other women.

The reporting can be sent via email to obiezione-respinta@autistiche.org or to the Obiezione Respinta Facebook page. Immediately after the launch of the map we decided to create a Facebook page to reach as many people as possible, and to create a digital space that was both an active space of resistance and a safe space to share experiences and testimonials.

The potential of the project surpassed our expectations. The page became a place for sharing competencies and knowledge thanks to the professionals who responded daily to the medical and legal questions of those people following and commenting on our articles. Furthermore, a large network of solidarity was born around Obiezione Respinta, which has united thousands of women. Connecting with others who have shared experiences defuses the guilt-mechanism and eliminates the feeling of loneliness that so often comes

---

7 Tecla InterActive, "Obiezione Vostro Onore," youtube video, Jan. 14, 2016. https://www.yout ube.com/watch?v=SDeZhYBCN0g.

8 Governmental report on the carrying out of law 194/78 – final data 2014 and 2015.

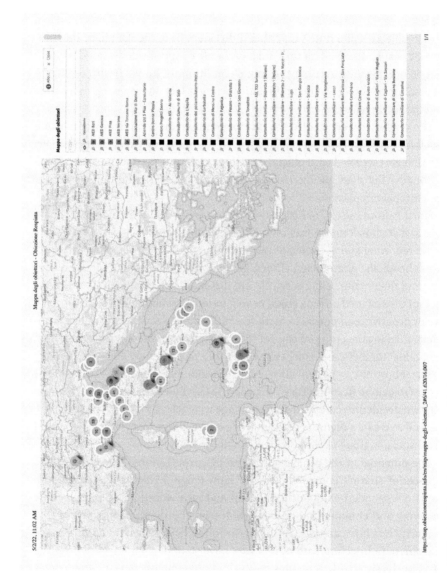

FIGURE 5.1 Map of conscientious objectors

FIGURE 5.2   Objection Denied chat site

after withstanding violence. There is no judgment, but rather support and reciprocal help between people who can be even hundreds of kilometers away but are linked by a keyboard and a screen.

The physical and virtual plans of vindication come together in the collective experience we shared during Non una di meno's mobilizing actions. The street protests and activist tabling about sexual and reproductive rights and health that took place on March 8th, 2017, energized the Facebook page, making it a national point of reference for signaling the presence of medical or pharmaceutical objectors. Today, the community is made up of almost ten thousand users while the map contains more than three hundred pins spread through every region of Italy.

One particular post clearly demonstrates the potential of the network to create emancipatory processes.

On July 23, 2017 a post was published with the testimony of a girl who, after what she herself deemed an "odyssey," was able to obtain the morning after pill in a pharmacy. In the office of Dr. Rossi and Dr. Magalotti the girl took a picture of a sign that said "for ethical-scientific reasons neither the morning after pill nor the 5 day pill are prescribed here." The image of the sign managed

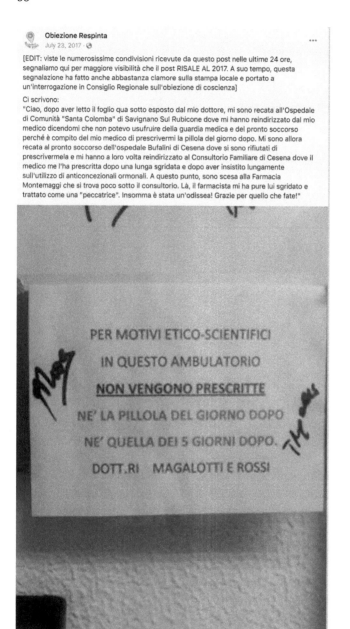

Obiezione Respinta
July 23, 2017 · 🌐

[EDIT: viste le numerosissime condivisioni ricevute da questo post nelle ultime 24 ore, segnaliamo qui per maggiore visibilità che il post RISALE AL 2017. A suo tempo, questa segnalazione ha fatto anche abbastanza clamore sulla stampa locale e portato a un'interrogazione in Consiglio Regionale sull'obiezione di coscienza]

Ci scrivono:
"Ciao, dopo aver letto il foglio qua sotto esposto dal mio dottore, mi sono recata all'Ospedale di Comunità "Santa Colomba" di Savignano Sul Rubicone dove mi hanno reindirizzato dal mio medico dicendomi che non potevo usufruire della guardia medica e del pronto soccorso perché è compito del mio medico di prescrivermi la pillola del giorno dopo. Mi sono allora recata al pronto soccorso dell'ospedale Bufalini di Cesena dove si sono rifiutati di prescrivermela e mi hanno a loro volta reindirizzato al Consultorio Familiare di Cesena dove il medico me l'ha prescritta dopo una lunga sgridata e dopo aver insistito lungamente sull'utilizzo di anticoncezionali ormonali. A questo punto, sono scesa alla Farmacia Montemaggi che si trova poco sotto il consultorio. Là, il farmacista mi ha pure lui sgridato e trattato come una "peccatrice". Insomma è stata un'odissea! Grazie per quello che fate!"

PER MOTIVI ETICO-SCIENTIFICI
IN QUESTO AMBULATORIO
NON VENGONO PRESCRITTE
NE' LA PILLOLA DEL GIORNO DOPO
NE' QUELLA DEI 5 GIORNI DOPO.
DOTT.RI   MAGALOTTI E ROSSI

😟👍❤️ 3.5K   2.3K Comments 1.9K Shares

👍 Like   💬 Comment   ↪ Share   ●▾

FIGURE 5.3   Facebook post recounting personal experience with
conscientious objector

to catalyze the attention of Facebook pages, online and print newspapers, and very quickly went viral. For the first time we realized we had ripped the cover off the mass-media silence that generally surrounds the stories we publish: shortly after the publication of the post, the medical board declared that they could denounce Dr. Magalotti; Piccinini, the regional advisor, publicly questioned the state of clinics in Emilia Romagna. The doctor was forced to remove the signage.

The interaction between the virtual plane, in which the unease caused by such violences is gathered and shared publicly, and the physical plane, in which the violence of medics and pharmacists operates, has pushed us to reflect on how to amplify these connections. Inquiring and analyzing the state of health services, we realized how insufficient and ill-equipped they are with respect to our needs. We have felt the need to set up gynecological and legal booths to aid all those who are usually excluded from national health services, and also to make autonomous transfeminist and queer spaces within which to question our common condition and expand on self-organizing strategies.

We realize the structural limits of this platform: while, on the one hand, thanks to "Obiezione Respinta," a woman can have more information about the presence of objectors, so as to avoid them; on the other hand, the objectors remain in the hospitals where women are still not able to decide about their own bodies. What goals should we give ourselves for the future? We believe that fighting in order to guarantee the sexual and reproductive health of each of us based on our need is the path to take.

Because when it comes to our bodies and our health, we decide!

Works Cited

Cubonix, Laboria and Helen Hester. *The Xenofeminist Manifesto*. New York: Verso, 2018.

Gemma, Rosella "Pillola del giorno dopo, Tribunale di Gorizia assolve farmacista obiettrice," Farmacista 33, December 20, 2016, www.farmacista33.it/pillola-del-giorno-dopo-tribunale-di-gorizia-assolve-farmacista-obiettrice/politica-e-sanita/news--38435.html?word=gorizia.

Tecla InterActive. "Obiezione Vostro Onore." Youtube video. Jan. 14, 2016. https://www.youtube.com/watch?v=SDeZhYBCNog.

CHAPTER 6

If I Was a Rich Girl

*Three Manifestos for Rethinking the Relationship between Gender,
Technology and Capital*

Elisa Virgili

At this point it is essentially taken for granted that the body must be in constant dialogue with technology, especially when it comes to biological sex, or rather, in the way it is distinguished as male or female. What is not presumed, however, is the way in which it does this, or, more specifically, the way it could do this. In what ways could bodies, particularly female bodies, use and not be used by technology?

This chapter will talk about these potentialities, starting with some fundamental reflections that have been made about the topic in the last few decades.

I start from an analysis of the ways Donna Haraway's *Cyborg Manifesto*[1] theorizes the relationship between technology and gender, and go on to consider implications for the current moment, paying attention to new reflections that have developed on the theme (beginning with Haraway but not only), and the technoeconomic changes of the last thirty years.

The premises needed to reappropriate technology and the notion of the cyborg are created by reflecting specifically on the critical issues involved in the figure of the cyborg and its implications for technocapitalism. The cyborg is redefined on the one hand, as an overcoming of the concept of gender–in the sense that for the cyborg gender differences are looser and assume different functions; and, on the other hand, it is redefined as a radical critique of capitalism (and thus of the concept of class), because it asks us to look at capitalism from an intersectional perspective, taking into account the various ways that gender, class, and race work on the subject.

The second step will be to look for Haraway's legacy and the legacy of reflections on the posthuman in *Accelerate Manifest for an Accelerationist Politics*,[2]

---

1   Donna Haraway, "A Cyborg Manifesto: Science, Technology, and Socialist-Feminism in the Late Twentieth Century," in Haraway, *Simians, Cyborgs, and Women: The Reinvention of Nature* (New York: Routledge, 1991), 149–181.

2   Alex Williams and Nick Srinicek, "#Accelerate Manifesto for an Accelerationist Politics," May 14, 2013, Critical Legal Thinking, https://criticallegalthinking.com/2013/05/14/accelerate -manifesto-for-an-accelerationist-politics/.

a text that problematizes the relationship between technology and capital, even if references to cyborg and queer theory are surprisingly absent given the premise from which it begins and the cultural tradition in which it is situated.

What is left of the body and of feminist reflection on it? We cannot exclude a critique of capitalism when thinking about the subject and about bodies, and this critique, in turn, cannot be separated from (cyborg)feminist thought, or rather, from a consideration of the relationship between technology and gender.

The third manifesto we will consider will be the *Xenofeminist Manifesto,*[3] which develops Haraway's theories on the relationship between technologies and the body using the new accelerationist critique that analyzes and proposes solutions for the effects of neoliberalism on subjects.

We will attempt an analysis of the *Xenofeminist Manifesto* in order to: see how these three points (gender, technology, capitalism) interact; understand if it is possible to use technology and capitalism in the service of subjects and their desires.

What these three manifestos share with much political theory is a reflection on the future. On the one hand this concept of technology is what links these manifestos, on the other it is the starting point from which to imagine political selfhood.

1   Cyborg Manifesto

I will begin by briefly mapping out the concept of the cyborg and more generally Donna Haraway's framing of it.

The *Manifesto* was published in the mid Eighties, following a period in which feminism was suspicious of science and technology because it regarded them as essentially patriarchal because they were fields largely dominated by men. During the time of the *Manifesto*'s publication feminists began discussing the role of women in the production of science–and women's access to technology–and consequently the role of science within feminism itself.[4]

What is missing from the conversation about women in science is the link between the problem in question and a broader reflection on society: one can

---

3 A version of the *Xenofeminist Manifesto* is in the original Italian edition of this book. Readers can find an English version here: Laboria Cubonix, *The Xenofeminist Manifesto,* (New York: Verso, 2018).

4 Sara Harding, *The Feminist Standpoint Theory Reader. Intellectual & Political Controversies,* (New York: Routledge, 2004).

clearly see a relationship of subordination, but no critical reflection has been done on the social, institutional, and economic apparatuses that grant access to that continued structure of power.

In the case of the role of science in feminism, however, all of these elements are taken into consideration, and this is precisely what makes this analysis a true political reflection.[5]

The analysis of the relationship between technology and the construction of gender becomes even more precise, and slowly reveals the mechanisms that need to be deconstructed. It is not just about how gender relates to technology; it is about how the former is constructed by the latter; and how technology is *just one* of the elements that constitute gender–along with class, race, sexual orientation and age (among others).

Decades ago, gender was proven to be a social construct, and now, with Haraway and Butler,[6] we have begun to see sex (understood as a biological fact) as a construct as well, and to consider nature and culture as not so completely distinguishable.

Technologies are also *engendered*. Particularly information and communication technologies, both from the point of view of production and their usage; they develop in relation to gender, a relationship in which one influences the other and vice versa.[7]

However, the subject does not passively endure its own construction; instead, it has a space of agency in which it is not a subjected subject but a subject that acts.

The theoretical fundamentals of these new ideas are Bruno Latour's *actor-network theory*, and constructionist theories. This is how the concept of technosociality is defined, referring to the material and semiotic formations, concrete objects and cultural apparatuses that constitute technology.

In the following decade these reflections became systematic and political in the narrowest sense. Thinkers like Plant and Turkle seem to trace a theory that is "animated by a naïve essentialism, that often trespasses into technological determinism, resulting in setting aside the historical and material dimensions of *wetware* in order to celebrate freedom without the limits of cyberspace."[8]

---

5 Evelyn Fox Keller, *Reflections on Gender and Science,* (New Haven: Yale University Press, 1985).

6 Judith Butler, *Gender Trouble,* (New York: Routledge, 1990).

7 Katherine Hayles, *How We Became Posthuman: Virtual Bodies in Cybernetics, Literature, and Informatics* (Chicago: University of Chicago Press, 1999).

8 Federica Timeto, "Per una teoria del cyberfemminismo oggi: dall'utopia tecnoscientifica alla critica situata del cyberspazio," in *Studi Culturali* anno VI, N. 3, Dec. 2009, p. 1.

Haraway's thinking should be positioned both along this path that has posed new lines of questioning and critique, and somewhere within continental philosophy. The roots of her theory can, in fact, be traced in part to French thinking about corporeal materialism. Canguilhem,[9] for example, says that in order to talk about the subject we must begin from its organic, carnal structure.

In Haraway, the concept of the human is redefined by its relationship with technology, but also by that which, over time, counts as human or, as Butler would say, by bodies that matter.[10]

Like Foucault,[11] Haraway's thinking places the emphasis on the construction of the subject and the manipulation of bodies. There is, however, a difference with regards to Foucault's analysis: power no longer acts through the same apparatuses he outlined; instead, it goes through networks, new modes of communication and new modalities of connection. It is a more updated version of the cartographies of power that are not always able to account for actualities.

Braidotti and Preciado also try to update the French thinker's analysis of the apparatuses of power that act on sexuality. The former uses the category of "posthuman zoe-politics" to describe the way in which "advanced capitalism" invades the sphere of biopolitics, acting on the genetic code of life within it, and in which subjects move from "free individuals" to "biogenetic dividuals."[12]

Preciado, on the other hand, uses the expression "pharmapornographic regime" to indicate the collection of apparatuses (contraceptive pills, commercial use of synthetic molecules, mass pornography) that "technocapitalism" uses to make a profit from, and regulate our lives.[13]

In these authors, the reflection on gender is accompanied by an understanding of technology and a knowledge of the economic dynamics that determine it.

> [T]o be in process or transition does not place the thinking subject outside history or time: postmodernity as a specific moment of our historicity is a major location that needs to be accounted for. A location is an

9   Georges Canguilhem, *The Normal and the Pathological*, (Turin: Einaudi, 1998).

10 Judith Butler, *Bodies that Matter: On the Discursive Limits of Sex*, (New York: Routledge, 1993).

11 Michel Foucault, *The History of Sexuality*, v.1, (New York: Pantheon Books, 1978).

12 Rosi Braidotti, *The Posthuman*, (Cambridge, UK: Polity Press, 2013). Lorenzo Bernini, "Pollyanna postumana desidera morire. L'eredità di Foucault tra affermatività femminista e negatività queer," in *Vita, politica, contingenza*, (Ancona: Quodlibet, 2016), 219–236.

13 Paul B. Preciado, *Testo Junkie. Sex, Drugs and Biopolitics in the Pharmacopornographic Era* (New York: Feminist Press, 2013).

embedded and embodied memory: it is a set of counter-memories, which are activated by the resisting thinker against the grain of dominant representations of subjectivity. A location is a materialist temporal and spatial site of co-production of the subject, and thus anything but an instance of relativism.[14]

Insofar as it is body-machine, the cyborg is a hybrid figure, it is a mechanism that can disrupt any binary, nature/culture, human/animal, male/female.

It is a material subject that is, at the same time, strengthened by a symbolic charge; born inside the same technological system it critiques; it is historically contingent upon and critical of liberal subjectivity.

It is essential to remember that the cyborg is a subject of *agency* that decides which categories it can embody and how it can remain within them, developing a politic that it chooses to articulate.

Like Butler's subject, and even before Foucault, the cyborg is able to thread its way through the interstices of the dominant apparatus. In the case of the technological one, by throwing into question the norm, it shows us a possibility of resistance.

Cyborgs are figurations of instability, not only between nature and culture, but also between ontology and epistemology.[15] Therefore, they challenge the definition of what nature is and what culture is, of what a machine is, human or animal (some Humanimal Studies, starting with Haraway, think through these concepts in interesting ways).

What does a cyborg have to do with gender? As Wendy Faulkner says, "both technology and gender [can] be understood as socially shaped and so potentially reshapable," or rather, both are an element that is "performed and processural in character, rather than given and unchanging."[16]

2   From Cyborg to Cyberfeminism

Within this panorama it is precisely the figure of the cyborg–at the heart of Donna Haraway's thinking–that is, in some way, absorbed within a general

---

14   Rosi Braidotti, Posthuman, "All Too Human: Towards a New Process Ontology," *Theory, Culture & Society*, 2006: 23(7–8):199.

15   Karen Barad, *Meeting the Universe Halfway. Quantum Physics and the Entanglement of Matter and Meaning*, (Durham: Duke University Press, 2007), 41.

16   Wendy Faulkner, "The Technology Question in Feminism. A View from Feminist Technology Studies," *Women's Studies International Forum* 21, no. 1 (2001): 80, 82.

political utopia that can be located in third wave, or postfeminism. In broad terms, their union gives life to cyberfeminism.

Just as with other feminisms, cyberfeminism has recently enriched itself with a new perspective that needs taking into account; namely, the economic one, understood not only as an aspect of class (which was already being considered), but also as a system of production and consumption.

It begins with the concept of situated knowledge (a knowledge that is born from a subject that belongs to a gender, a class, etc., and that, in some way, is influenced by the position in which it finds itself) that Haraway develops and reflects on information and communication technologies that are increasingly more important both in the technological and economic spheres.

Beginning in the early Nineties, cyberfeminism carries out analyses on the relationship between gender and technology both in theory and in practice.[17]

Haraway lends us a feminist critique that engages but does not detach from technology; however, what seems to get lost is the question of the subject's socio-economic positionality and thus of the political valence of Haraway's theory.

The other part of cyberfeminism, instead, tries to think about the body in its materiality, in its immanence; conditions that include technology and its accessibility.

Technology and scientific progress do not automatically guarantee autonomy and liberty for the subject, there are other sides of our lives that remain blocked between borders, prohibitive normativities and exorbitantly priced markets.[18]

"Technology isn't inherently progressive. Its uses are fused with culture in a positive feedback loop that makes linear sequencing, prediction, and absolute caution impossible. Technoscientific innovation must be linked to a collective theoretical and political thinking in which women, queers, and the gender non-conforming play an unparalleled role" as they say in the *Xenofeminist Manifesto*.[19]

---

17 The origin of the term cyberfeminism dates back to the beginning of the Nineties and is attributed alternatively to the Australian artist group VNS Matrix8 that, in 1991 published the first cyberfeminist manifesto, and to a series of theoretical writings by Sadie Plant who, at more or less the same time, began to use this terminology to indicate the alliance between women, machines and new technologies. The institutionalization of cyberfeminism is traced back to the conference "Seduced and Abandoned: The Body in the Virtual World," that took place in London at the Institute of Contemporary Art in 1994.

18 Angela Balzano, "Le conseguenze dell'amore ai tempi del biocapitalismo. Diritti riproduttivi e mercati della fertilità," in *Il genere tra neoliberalismo e neofondamentalismo*, edited by Zappino Federico, (Verona: Ombre Corte, 2016), 110–125.

19 Cuboniks, *Xenofeminist*, 2.

We can't forget that the cyborg is a corporeal being; we cannot fall into the Cartesian trap that makes us forget our bodies in order to forget the bodies of minorities.

Sadie Plant emphasizes the web as a tool for deconstructing the economy and the patriarchal order.[20] Instead of being squashed, in this context women are able to gain some advantage from new technologies. To use Deleuzian philosophy, becoming a woman in this context is the–never completed–result of the procedurality itself of the web, and it has nothing to do with any identity claims. The bodies, like Haraway's cyborgs, always remain between categories, between receptacles; but once again we are missing the political element, missing the agency of the subject.

However, cyberfeminism proposes its own self-critique at the end of the Nineties, in the same years that it begins to carry a certain weight in academic and artistic spheres. It begins, therefore, to reflect on other dimensions and vectors of power related to gender and technology, such as class and race (maybe generally coinciding with a certain intersectional feminism).

The subject is once again situated: the necessity of positioning oneself politically and epistemologically, the situation of the situated.[21]

The criticism, therefore, aims at cyberliberationist thought that often coincides with the ideals of neoliberalism, and sees technological development as predetermined and directed toward positive progress *a priori*.

We sustain Braidotti's claim that capitalism "produces a paradoxical and rather opportunistic form of post-anthropocentrism on the part of market forces which happily trade on life itself."[22] I believe that with these three manifestos it comes down to imagining the future, thinking about the subject in the future; it is difficult for a political philosophy, or theory in general, not to think about the subject located in time.

---

20   Sadie Plant, "On the Matrix. Cyberfeminist Simulations," in *The Gendered Cyborg. A Reader*, edited by Gill Kirkup, Linda Janes, Kath Woodward, and Fiona Hovenden, (New York: Routledge, 2001) 265–275.

21   Donna Haraway, "Situated Knowledges: The Science Question in Feminism and the Privilege of Partial Perspective," *Feminist Studies* 14, no. 3 (1988): 575–99.

22   Rosi Braidotti, "Posthuman Affirmative Politics" in *Resisting Biopolitics: Philosophical, Political and Performative Strategies*, eds. S.E. Wilmer and Audrone Zukauskaite (New York: Routledge, 2016), 42.

3   Accelerationist Manifesto

Manifesto for an Accelerationist Politics (*Mpa*) presents a reflection on technology and, specifically, on its relationship to capital; it begins with a consideration of the existing crisis and an analysis of its causes, foremost among these "the increasing automation in production processes," which include intellectual or cognitive labor, understood (in simple terms) as every form of work that produces knowledge and that uses this knowledge to generate meaning and to govern and enact material transformations realized by machines and by artificial labor.

Published in 2013 by Alex Williams and Nick Srnicek, and translated into various languages, *Mpa* is born from the intellectual environment created around the journal *Collapse*, and refers, in part, to the genre of philosophy known as "speculative realism," the main authors of which are Reza Negarestani and Ray Brassier.

The *Manifesto* gave life to a proliferation of papers and conferences on the topic and, in 2015, the authors published a book, *Inventing the Future*, in which the accelerationist proposal was systematically laid out.

Mpa's twenty-four point thesis is that one must act within the capitalist system itself, accelerating economic and technological development which, consequently, creates an increase in the divide between the social classes. In this way, the *Manifesto* reclaims something of the tradition of the center-right worker.[23]

The concept of acceleration should not, however, be confused with that of velocity, given that the former is a creative process that develops within the interstices left uncovered by the productive capitalist system, whereas the latter is simply production at a greater speed. Therefore, it is about liberating the latent forces of cognitive labor and imagining another type of work.

> Whereas the techno-utopians argue for acceleration on the basis that it will automatically overcome social conflict, our position is that technology should be accelerated precisely because it is needed to win social conflicts.[24]

---

23   Antonio Negri, "Riflessioni sul "manifesto per una politica accelerazionista," in *Gli algoritmi del capitale*, (Verona: Ombre Corte, 2014).

24   Williams and Srnicek, "#Accelerate Manifesto for an Accelerationist Politics.".

As we have seen occur with cyberfeminist critique, technology in and of itself is not used as a positive or a negative; instead, its uses are what determine its role in politics.

Citing Deleuze, we can affirm that, "each kind of society corresponds to a particular kind of machine–with simple mechanical machines corresponding to sovereign societies, thermo-dynamic machines to disciplinary societies, cybernetic machines and computers to control societies. But the machines don't explain anything, you have to analyze the collective arrangements of which the machines are just one component."[25]

Technology is a *pharmakon*, a cure and a poison at the same time, and it is constitutive of being human in the way in which it reveals humans' non-constitutive essence and essential incompleteness, given that one cannot think about man without technology, or nature without culture.

At the base of this manifesto there seems to be a reflection on the relationship between being human and technology, in which the fundamental question is not so much what we want to accelerate, but *who* is doing the accelerating and who is accelerating *themselves*.

Like cyberfeminism, the *Mpa* does not forget that the subject in question is a body, and it reflects on the material qualities and techniques of the corporeal reappropriation of fixed capital (information is currently the most highly valued), and on the subsequent anthropological transformation of the worker-subject. All new productive processes tied to more modern technologies (for instance, the analysis of *big data*) have the possibility of being re-elaborated and reappropriated by worker-subjects.

To this end, Guattari, in *Caosmosi*, already talked about a postmediatic lens within which an explosion of media control–marked by a proliferation of collective agents of enunciation and by a reappropriation of media use–would occur, though not without its problems.

As subjects, we constantly interact with algorithms that regulate our relationship with data and digital devices, as well as with systems of logic, medicine, urban planning, and many other techniques with which our bodies come into contact.

As Cinquemani and De Majo observe, "it is possible to think that electro-computational atomization governed by algorithms involves an already hybridized body-space, a living mechanical network that involves the living,

---

25   Gilles Deleuze and Antonio Negri, "Deleuze Control and Becoming: A Conversation Between Toni Negri and Gilles Deleuze," The Funabulist, February 22, 2011, https://the funambulist.net/editorials/philosophy-control-and-becoming-a-conversation-between -toni-negri-and-gilles-deleuze.

the infrastructures of communication and digital networks; a complex apparatus of automated-subjection at the base of which we find the algorithmic component."[26]

The body in question is Deleuze and Guattari's "body without organs," it is a body that has a relationship to modernity and resists the total regulation embodied within the productive body. It is a body whose borders are never fully defined and leave space for creation and imagination.[27]

In the fourth point of the *Mpa* the attention to the body becomes an attention to a sexed body: "We do not want to return to Fordism. There can be no return to Fordism. The capitalist 'golden era' was premised on the production paradigm of the orderly factory environment, where (male) workers received security and a basic standard of living in return for a lifetime of stultifying boredom and social repression. Such a system relied upon an international hierarchy of colonies, empires, and an underdeveloped periphery; a national hierarchy of racism and sexism; and a rigid family hierarchy of female subjugation. For all the nostalgia many may feel, this regime is both undesirable and practically impossible to return to."[28]

The constant attempt by these grammatizations to capture desire seems bankrupt to us. Sexed bodies resist discipline and heteronormativity, as we have seen from recent queer movements that have also known how to use digital technology to their advantage.

But they are also bodies that fill streets and public squares, that have used technology to weave together relationships and initiate social movements.[29] Body and technology have never been this hybrid, the border between the single body, the collective, and digital technologies is fragmented to produce resistance.

4   Xenofeminist Manifesto

Even though the *Mpa* explicitly considers the body as sexed, this reflection is limited to just one part of the problem, and the analyses that followed the

---

26   Luca Cinquemani and Eleonora de Majo, *Grammatizzazioni dello spazio corpo: tra algoritmizzazione ed eccedenze*, (Palermo: University of Palermo, 2015),13.

27   Tiziani Villani, "Body," in *Lessico postfordista. Dizionario di idee della mutazione*, edited by Adelino Zanini and Ubaldo Fadini (Milan: Feltrinelli, 2001), 76–80.

28   Williams and Srnicek, "#Accelerate Manifesto for an Accelerationist Politics.".

29   Saskia Sassen, *Territorio, autorità e diritti. Assemblaggi dal Medioevo all'era globale*, (Milan: Mondadori, 2008).

publication of the manifesto seem to have ignored this, or at least they seem neither to have developed this aspect, nor to have considered it fundamental.

There are those who inherited both Haraway's and the accelerationist thoughts: they are the *Xenofeminist Manifesto*.

The manifesto is written by Laboria Cuboniks, an anagram of the pseudonym Nicolas Bourbaki, a collective formed by six women who developed xenofeminist theory, characterized in part by scholars as a branch of accelerationism, an anticapitalist feminism that highlights not just the oppression of gender, but also the various forms of oppression created by capitalism, that can currently be understood as oppression enacted through the diversity of economic resources available and the different geographical placement of the subjects involved.

Even if neoliberalism today seems preoccupied with gender dynamics, it continues to situate itself within an oppressive system, both when it takes the form of businesses that have a policy on gender equality, and when it relates to a certain postfeminism depicted, for the most part, by blogs and pop stars who give voice to a "women's" liberation that is seen more as a personal, individual realization than as a collective movement.

The neoliberal proposal tries to integrate every oppressed group (women, LGBTQ) within the same neoliberal system; it does nothing other than create other oppressed groups.

Can one, therefore, have a feminism that, in the name of integration, excludes other subjects?

In my opinion xenofeminism tries to deconstruct this included/excluded binary, by collapsing the capitalist system, starting with the reappropriation of its technological resources.

The only way to destroy capitalism, from this point of view, is with the tools capitalism itself offers (digital technology and digital culture), just as accelerationism tells us.

One of the principal goals, as we can read in the beginning of the *Manifesto*, is liberation from the "drudgery of labor, both productive and reproductive;" a double gender liberation. It is about liberating oneself from productive labor (in the sense of producing goods), but also familial labor; and, at the same time, it proposes conceiving of new family models, different in their composition, that liberate us from the repetitive time of domestic and extra-domestic labor.

In this sense, the *Xenofeminist Manifesto* is an attempt to answer the question: what part of accelerationism has to do with leftist feminism?

Both accelerationism and leftist feminism view technology and progress not as liberatory *per se*. The manifesto examines the criticality of technology and looks for spaces where eccentric subjects can insert themselves.

It is a feminism that looks to the future and has a long-term plan.

There is a long history between feminism and the image of the future, one told very well by feminist science fiction. The *Xenofeminist Manifesto* tells us that these stories are not so far off or impossible, that reappropriating technology could really go in our favor.

It is a cunning feminism, just as the collective itself defines it, and not, I will add, a feminism of reason, as reason and rationalism have for so long been fundamental to Western (male) thought, and often the enemy of feminism and feminist thought. It is a cunning feminism because it steals the tools of its oppressor to defeat him.

The authors themselves define the *Manifesto* as feminist, technomaterialist, antinaturist and abolitionist of gender.

It is technomaterialist in its belief that the majority of existing scientific research and technology is not simply beneficial to society. The *Manifesto* reflects critically on the use of technology, on how this use is not at all neutral, nor are its subjects that invent and construct it. The question is also posed the other way around, namely: who has access to this technology and at what price?

It is antinaturist because "Anyone who's been deemed 'unnatural' in the face of reigning biological norms, anyone who's experienced injustices wrought in the name of natural order, will realize that the glorification of 'nature' has nothing to offer us–the queer and trans among us, the differently-abled, as well as those who have suffered discrimination due to pregnancy or duties connected to child-rearing."[30]

The critique of nature is, here, a critique of heteronormativity: if being heterosexual is considered natural, it is because it goes hand in hand with the norm (understood as law and at the same time as normality); a norm that is created through its very repetition. Spaces are created between one repetition and another, spaces in which we can act and destabilize the norm and, in this way, demonstrate that is it not natural, that one is not heterosexual by nature, but that nature was constructed a posteriori by the repetition of the norm.

This adds to an intersectional critique that both takes on different vectors of power not limited to gender or sexuality, and, as we have already said, affirms that there cannot be liberation from gender oppression that leaves behind those who are oppressed on account of their economic condition, social position, skin color, or sexual orientation.

It is antinaturist if, by nature we mean that biological determinism that brings about gender inequality, that nature that equates normal with natural;

---

30   Cuboniks, *Xenofeminist,* 1.

it is this antinaturist stance which produces the abolition of gender. The same conversation about heteronormativity also holds true for bodies, for biological sex that, it seems, can only ever be reduced to binaries. That a person is biologically defined as male or female is not a natural biological fact; rather, it is the interpretation of sciences like medicine and biology. There are subjects, intersexed persons, for instance, who do not fit into any of the established categories and not because they are not natural, but because parameters have been established that render a body male or female; these are not natural parameters, they come from the medical manuals. What happens if we modify these manuals? What happens if we reappropriate this scientific knowledge for ourselves, and take back the technologies it uses to force bodies into these preset binaries?

Xenofeminism is located, in other words, within a certain queer thinking that, since the early Nineties, began questioning the fact the not only gender but also, in some way, sex is a social construct.

In particular, it can be put in dialogue with the theories of Preciado. Preciado coined the term "pharmapornographic regime" to describe the process through which, beginning in the Fifties, a series of biotechnological developments renewed the tools "technocapitalism" uses to govern, exploit and profit from a life and that, both in theory and in practice, reappropriated technology (specifically, in the case of hormonal therapies).

It is about abolishing gender not because gender should no longer exist, but because there can be many, because the stereotypical constructions of masculine and feminine can be modified, and, above all, because the construction of gender is no longer tied to the asymmetrical operation of power.

The abolition of race follows a similar path to arrive at a point where the racial characteristics of a subject are no longer the basis for discrimination.

The *Manifesto* also does away with the stark division between the virtual and real: most of the points I've discussed thus far seem to deal with material questions, however, much of the technology that surrounds us today is digital technology, tied to the virtual world. The material and the virtual are linked and of equal importance, one cannot act on material reality without thinking about the digital technology that acts on the representation of the self.

Xenofeminism offers itself not simply as a horizontal platform, but also a molecular one, that can build new languages and practices of sexual politics and can *change nature.*

5   Conclusions

After a period in which politics cast its gaze backward, and the word of the day was nostalgia, the "official" narratives have begun to abuse the concept of the future. Lately, in Italy in particular, the rhetoric tells us that what is past is old, negative, and to be discarded. The future that the *Accelerationist Manifesto* and the *Xenofeminist Manifesto* speak of is a different future, a time of acceleration.

All three manifestos offer instruments for building a future in which all bodies matter. But theirs isn't a pacifying utopia; it will be a future of conflicts, anything but conciliatory.

Works Cited

Balzano, Angela, "Le conseguenze dell'amore ai tempi del biocapitalismo. Diritti riproduttivi e mercati della fertilità." In *Il genere tra neoliberalismo e neofondamentalismo.* Edited by Zappino Federico, 110–125. Verona: Ombre Corte, 2016.

Barad, Karen. *Meeting the Universe Halfway. Quantum Physics and the Entanglement of Matter and Meaning.* Durham: Duke University Press, 2007.

Bernini, Lorenzo. "Pollyanna postumana desidera morire. L'eredità di foucault tra affermatività femminista e negatività queer." In *Vita, politica, contingenza,* 219–236. Ancona: Quodlibet, 2016.

Braidotti, Rosi. "All Too Human: Towards a New Process Ontology." *Theory, Culture & Society.* 2006: 23(7–8):197–208.

Braidotti, Rosi. *The Posthuman.* Cambridge, UK: Polity Press, 2013.

Braidotti, Rosi. "Posthuman Affirmative Politics." In *Resisting Biopolitics: Philosophical, Political and Performative Strategies.* Ed.s S.E. Wilmer and Audrone Zukauskaite, 30–56. New York: Routledge, 2016.

Butler, Judith. *Gender Trouble: Feminism and the Subversion of Identity.* New York: Routledge, 1990.

Butler, Judith. *Bodies that Matter: On the Discursive Limits of Sex.* New York: Routledge, 1993.

Canguilhem, Georges. *The Normal and the Pathological.* Turin: Einaudi, 1998.

Cubonix, Laboria and Helen Hester. *The Xenofeminist Manifesto.* New York: Verso, 2018.

Cinquemani, Luca and Eleonora de Majo. *Grammatizzazioni dello spazio corpo: tra algoritmizzazione ed eccedenze.* Palermo: University of Palermo, 2015.

Deleuze, Gilles and Antonio Negri. "Deleuze Control and Becoming: A Conversation Between Faulkner, Wendy. "The Technology Question in Feminism. A View from Feminist Technology Studies." *Women's Studies International Forum* 21, no. 1 (2001):79–95.

Foucault, Michel. *The History of Sexuality*, v.1. New York: Pantheon Books, 1978.

Haraway, Donna. "A Cyborg Manifesto: Science, Technology, and Socialist-Feminism in the Late Twentieth Century." In *Simians, Cyborgs, and Women: The Reinvention of Nature,* Haraway, 149–181. New York: Routledge, 1991.

Harding, Sara. *The Feminist Standpoint Theory Reader. Intellectual & Political Controversies.* New York: Routledge, 2004.

Hayles, Katherine. *How We Became Posthuman: Virtual Bodies in Cybernetics, Literature, and Informatics.* Chicago: University of Chicago Press, 1999.

Keller, Evelyn Fox. *Reflections on Gender and Science.* New Haven: Yale University Press, 1985.

Negri, Antonio. "Riflessioni sul "manifesto per una politica accelerazionista." In *Gli algoritmi del capitale.* Verona: Ombre Corte, 2014.

Negri, Antonio and Gilles Deleuze." The Funabulist, February 22, 2011. https://thefuna mbulist.net/editorials/philosophy-control-and-becoming-a-conversation-betw een-toni-negri-and-gilles-deleuze.

Plant, Sadie. "On The Matrix. Cyberfeminist Simulations." In *The Gendered Cyborg. A Reader.* Ed.s by Gill Kirkup, Linda Janes, Kath Woodward, and Fiona Hovenden, 265–275. New York: Routledge, 2001.

Preciado, Paul B. *Testo Junkie. Sex, Drugs and Biopolitics in the Pharmacopornographic Era.* New York: Feminist Press, 2013.

Sassen, Saskia. *Territorio, autorità e diritti. Assemblaggi dal Medioevo all'era globale.* Milan: Mondadori, 2008.

Timeto, Federica. "Per una teoria del cyberfemminismo oggi: dall'utopia tecnoscienti-fica alla critica situata del cyberspazio." *Studi Culturali* anno VI, N. 3, Dec. 2009: 1–26.

Villani, Tiziani. "Body." In *Lessico postfordista. Dizionario di idee della mutazione.* Edited by Adelino Zanini and Ubaldo Fadini, 76–80. Milan: Feltrinelli, 2001.

Wajcman, Judy. *TechnoFeminism.* Cambridge: Polity, 2004.

Williams, Alex and Nick Srinicek. "#Accelerate Manifesto for an Accelerationist Politics." May 14, 2013. Critical Legal Thinking. https://criticallegalthinking.com/ 2013/05/14/accelerate-manifesto-for-an-accelerationist-politics/.

eva kunin * Arigato (Gozaimasu) ebook

eva kunin

FIGURE 7.1   QR code 1

1   From the Real to the Virtual

eva kunin's Arigato (gozaimasu) ebook began in 2012 as a *digital editorial performance* based on *Deleuze's* notion of *cartography*. The author, *eva kunin*, is a queer digital identity project that explores the potential of new technologies in "constructing" other identities.

According to *eva kunin*, we create spaces when we think.

When we live and recount our experiences to one another, we create space. *Deleuze* explains it very well, describing desire as a space: what we desire is not something or someone, it is a space in our minds that something or someone helps build.[1]

We are, without a doubt, builders/architects/performers of our own reality, so it is fundamental that we are equipped to create our own maps, our own "existential" cartographies that are able to help us narrate and interpret our reality/our desires in every phase of life, each in their own complexity.

The *arigato (gozaimasu) ebook* project is precisely this: an ebook that, by exploiting the possibilities of digital tools 2.0, experiments with the creation of a *digital cartography of the real*; a narrative geography that started as an *open content* link containing various multimediatic hyperlinks.

If, as Deleuze affirms, *cartography* is a map with infinite entrances and exits that are in a state of continuous becoming, then digital writing with all its potentially infinite rhizomatic *connections/links* (entrances-exits), seems like the best choice for writing this map. The book is presented, therefore, as

---

1   eva kunin, "Deleuze Desir," youtube video, Sept.16 2019 https://youtube.com/playlist?list=PLo-m5UQZcTiRaOMIyx9coECMVTBojW7GH.

a *hypertext-container,* a multilayered text: a *reading movement* that resembles a "neighborhood walk" *without a center (parkour).* It goes beyond the traditional book-reader binary relationship and, for this exact reason, seems like the best option for telling a story with a *queer* theme: a little spatiotemporal fragment of reality that goes beyond the binaries of man-woman, male-female and, more generally, beyond the heteronormativity that surrounds us.

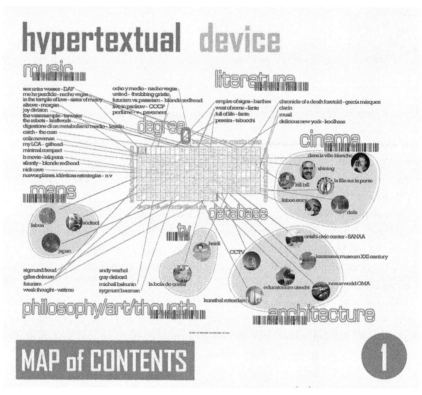

FIGURE 7.2   Map of contents

The entire project is laid out as a *rhizome of digital tools* that operate in synergy and contribute to the creation and becoming of the cartography that make up this rhizome. Thusly, *arigato (gozaimasu) ebook* is:

1.   A website: arigatoebook.com
2.   A map downloaded from the ebook and updated in real time
3.   A guerilla marketing campaign that uses QR code stickers
4.   Two FB pages

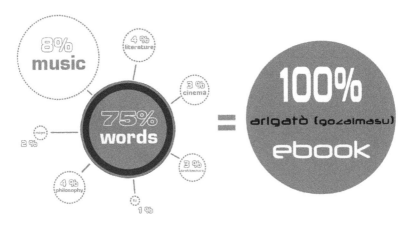

FIGURE 7.3   Diagram of multimedia content

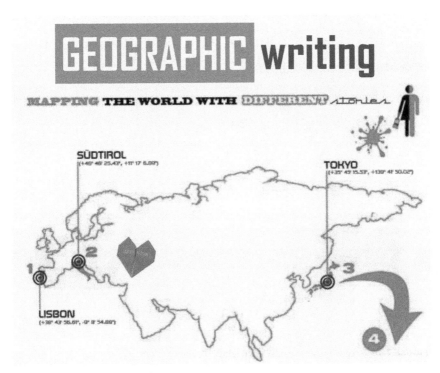

FIGURE 7.4   Text-related Google Map

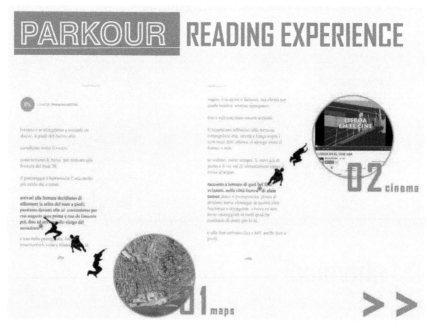

FIGURE 7.5   Parkour-inspired centerless reading, diagram 1

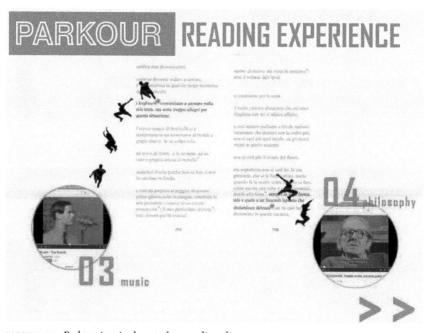

FIGURE 7.6   Parkour-inspired centerless reading, diagram 2

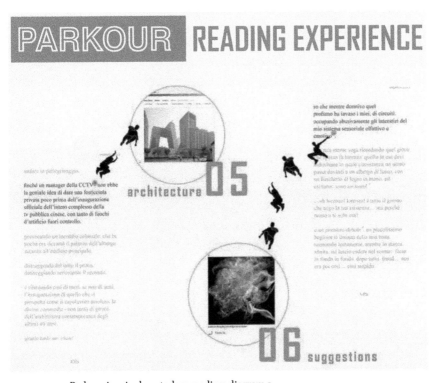

FIGURE 7.7   Parkour-inspired centerless reading, diagram 3

FIGURE 7.8   QR code 2

FIGURE 7.9   Map to download eBook

FIGURE 7.10 Guerilla marketing campaign images 1

FIGURE 7.11   Guerilla marketing campaign images 2

FIGURE 7.12   eBook Facebook page

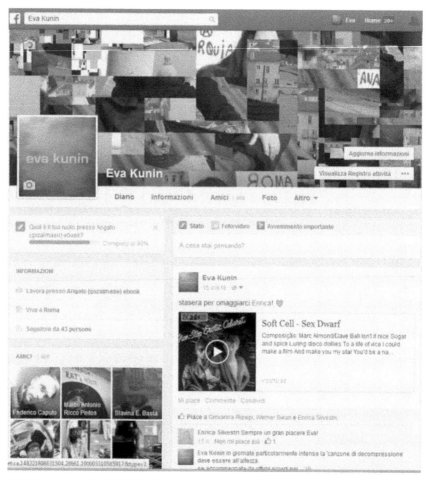

FIGURE 7.13   eva kunin Facebook page

5.   A virtual identity in the figure of *eva kunin* who is an *in-between* identity
     space that exists between the binarisms of real-virtual/male-female and,
     as we've said, an attempt to explore the potential of new technologies in
     "constructing" identities beyond preestablished binaries.

2   From the Virtual to the Real

2.1   *Supernova* (*Narrative Cartography of a Queer Space*)
Just as with every intensely virtual project, arigato (gozaimasu) ebook ran the
risk of remaining "disconnected" from reality when one of its initial intentions
was the ability to contribute to changing this reality.

The guerilla marketing campaign of QR codes and the various presentations of the project in its first years of life were attempts to correct for this risk.

But what was likely the most important experience in the attempt to bring this project into reality was the building of a NARRATIVE CARTOGRAPHY *of a* QUEER SPACE; namely, an *emotional-situationist* stroll in the Pigneto neighborhood of Rome in *September of 2015* as part of *arigato (gozaimasu) ebook* project's participation in the III *Geographies of Sexuality Conference.*

The Pigneto neighborhood, by now a fairly central area, is a former Roman hamlet at the southeastern edge of the Aurelian wall; it is a neighborhood that has already been narrated by one who could be considered among the first *queer cartographers: P.P. Pasolini.*[2] Today it is a complex and contradictory neighborhood, crisscrossed by a variety of dynamics and interests that are often at odds with one another: from gentrification to blatant drug dealing, and all the shades of gray one can imagine in between these opposing phenomena.

A different cartography was traced in this complex context in order to shed light on one of the many precious threads (*queer* in this case) that shape the rich, variegated social fabric that still resists/exists in Pigneto.

Let's begin with a chapter in *arigato (gozaimasu) ebook* written by *Francesca Feola* for the occasion: SUPERNOVA, a stroll that takes place in Pigneto. This piece was thought of as a QR code "treasure hunt" that led us to multimedia content which allowed us to follow the narration in real time.

FIGURE 7.14 QR code 3

Participants were given an origami-map with the stops of the journey and QR codes that redirect to narrative content.

Together, the group moved through the neighborhood streets using a radio to listen to the pieces created for the occasion by the event's collaborators: the *Zarra Bonheur (Rachele Borghi,* performer and professor of Geography of Sexuality at the Sorbonne University in Paris, and *Slavina,* postporn activist), *Francesca Feola,* queer activist and author of *Supernova,* and *Barbara de Vivo,* queer activist and long-time neighborhood resident, and *eva kunin.*

---

2   Pier Paolo Pasolini was a queer painter, filmmaker, writer and intellectual whose work often deals with questions of sexuality and marginalization. One of his early films is situated in the Pigneto neighborhood (*Accattone,* 1961).

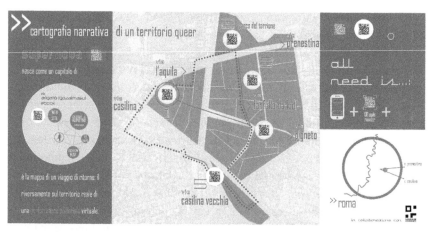

FIGURE 7.15   Queer territory narrative map

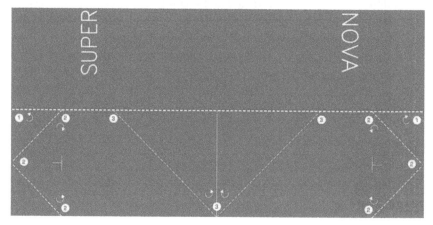

FIGURE 7.16   Super nova

This collective movement through the streets of the neighborhood while listening together to different original pieces, had a double purpose:
– On the one hand, there was the *experiential* intention on the individual level: listening to a text in places where the action unfolded allowed participants to live the experience sensorially with a certain level of intensity;
– On the other hand, there was a *performative collective* intention: moving as a "*queer* group," in the daytime through the streets of a specific urban space helped underline, signal and bring to light a social group that makes up the neighborhood but that typically lives it at different times of day; this stroll changed the "landscape" and, at least temporarily, improved it and narrated

FIGURE 7.17   Fingers touching QR code

FIGURE 7.18 Gender symbol

it with "a renewed awareness of the relationship between the self and public space: a way to *confront the (hetero)norms that govern it.*"[3]

3   Interview with Rachele Borghi in March 2015.

CHAPTER 8

Notes from the Center's Margins

Rachele Borghi (Zarra Bonheur)

1 Separate

In her famous 1989 text, bell hooks approaches the theme of marginalization from an original perspective. Her reading of the margin as a space of resistance and a radical place of possibility offers an empowering vision of marginalization, which is seen as a space of creation and not one of submission.[1] This inversion of perspective allows us to think of the margin as a space to inhabit, a space in which to find one's place, a place to *stay* and not just as a transitional space to occupy as you wait to reach the center. This is a crucial epistemological change: the margins become spaces of creation, of sharing, of elaborating collective strategies, of counter-spaces,[2] of mapping out new ways of looking at the world. The margin as a counter-hegemonic space is the place to share experiences, situations, and life journeys. Marginalization is thus not just a privileged space for creating, it is also a space from which to adopt a *privileged* perspective on the world. What is invisible becomes visible, social values and processes that have been internalized become denaturalized, the mechanisms that work to maintain the dominant system become explicit.

The margin thus becomes the privileged space for the elaboration of viral micro-politics, the space for counter-attack.

2 Context

The reflections that follow are the product of experimental practices that started from the margins of a center-space, or rather, a central space within a dominant system; a space that is fundamental for maintaining its order, and directly implicated in the reproduction of mechanisms of power and relationships of domination: the university.

---

1 bell hooks, *Yearnings: Race, Gender and Cultural Politics*, (Boston: South and Press, 1989).
2 Michel Foucault, "Other Spaces," in *Architecture, Movement, Continuity* 1, no. 5 (1984):46–49.

The French (and Italian) academic space strongly resists the perpetuation of critical epistemologies. Not only is the positivist paradigm (the norm of scientific production) very present, it gives life to forms of epistemic violence that prevent the development of an epistemological creativity geared toward social transformation instead of social objectification.[3]

The university is a privileged space for the exercising of institutional power. A citadel. This is because, figuratively, it closes in on itself, and becomes inaccessible to society, while discourses on opennesss, on the creation of bridges between university education and society/the workforce become increasingly neoliberal.[4]

The university can also become a prison, a space of self-confinement. When you are part of an institution, you often internalize the idea that there are certain actions/practices/ideas/subjects/questions that you can achieve/face and others that, to the contrary, are out of place,[5] as is the subject proposing them. In this way, praxes are created based on the more or less conscious internalization of norms, producing self-imposed and self-managed restrictions.

Is it possible to transgress these praxes? When you are a part of an institution, when your body *is* the teaching institutional body, how much room is there to resist the order imposed by the institution?

While it is true that "the master's tools will never dismantle the master's house,"[6] one can perhaps penetrate the master's house, slip through a crack, wedge oneself in a crevice and set up camp. When, because of a series of circumstances, you manage to do it, then, from there, you can maintain a privileged point/position from which to look and begin to contaminate spaces. Starting from that space, it is thus possible to learn to surpass, to contain, to bypass, to overturn the institutional norms and rules. Necessary conditions: a) renounce approval, recognition of one's own legitimacy, and of being accepted; b) endure the exhaustion that comes with occupying the interstice; c) reverse the negative value of "remaining in the margins" to live the freedom and the creativity in inhabiting them.

3   Rachele Borghi, Sam/Marie-Hélène Bourcier, and Cha Prieur, "Performing Academy: Feedback and Diffusion Strategies for Queer Researchers," in *The Routledge Research Companion to Geographies of Sex and Sexualities,* edited by Gavin Brown and Kath Browne (London: Routledge, 2016), p. 165.

4   Sam/Marie-Hélène Bourcier, *Homo.inc* (Paris: Cambourakis, 2017).

5   Tim Cresswell, *In Place/Out of Place. Geography, Ideology, and Transgression* (Minneapolis: University of Minnesota Press, 1996).

6   Audre Lorde, *Sister Outsider,* (New York: Crossing Press, 1984), 110–114.

Self-control and self-censorship are two powerful apparatuses. Freedom to teach and research, and the lack of apparatuses of control over the content of our courses gives the individual instructor autonomy. It is the self-control and self-censorship, or rather self-governing mentality that makes the reiteration of the dominant praxes (of epistemological teaching and research) possible within a given context. Attempting to free oneself requires enormous effort. To be public about your minority practices and epistemes reveals your fragility. Added to the exhaustion of this labor is the supplemental labor of scientific research that will construct a solid theoretical framework that is impregnable; it is much more exhausting than what is required of those whose praxes refer to a dominant paradigm. Hours of unpaid and unacknowledged overtime to defend one's theoretic references, course schedules, and methodological and bibliographical choices so that their legitimacy is recognized by students.

Despite all this, creating and experimenting with forms of resistance to the norms imposed by dominant subjects in the context of the institution is possible.

3   Chapter 1. The Body of/in the Field

In the last few years my research has focused on how the body enters in relation to space. The body in itself represents a space, and the social dynamics that have their own spatial solidification in bodies. The body is a space where performance comes alive and has worth as a tool of resistance and rupture of the norms that regulate public spaces. From this perspective the body can become a tool for the transgression of dominant social norms in a determined space. Starting from these considerations, I became interested in postporno[7] as a militant sexual dissidence movement. Postporno seemed to me a material, corporeal actualization of queer theories, and a strong example of breaking norms through the body. I began to study postporno performances created in public, and their relationship to these places. The method of ethnographic research that I practiced required my direct participation in the workshops. In the transfeminist postporno context, workshops are privileged spaces for the

---

7   Postporno breaks from those binaries through which sexuality is represented and performed, in order to stress its political worth, and remove itself from the confines of the private sphere. This is a fluid phenomenon that attempts to free itself of every label. The protagonists themselves are the ones to define it "postporno;" at the same time, however, they refuse the idea of participating in a homogeneous movement, and some even of participating in a collective, formed through common, definable, and clearly delineated traits.

flow, sharing, and creation of collective knowledges. I participated in bondage, *squirting* (theory-practices), reading, writing, sex toy production, and BDSM (bondage, domination, submission, sadomasochism) workshops. It was all new to me, and what was especially new was the fact that my body occupied a central position in the field. My body was no longer what took me around the field, it had become *my* field. I had to confront values that my very normed body conveyed in an anarcho-punk context that was initially foreign to me, and reflect on my legitimacy in *being* there, and working in/on that context, on my methods, and on my research practices.

It wasn't enough to make my position explicit each time. The gesture of taking notes, and my having a notebook, marked my body in that space, much more than taking pictures or filming, since they were contexts in which the visual and technological prostheses are very present.

I have thought a lot about the way I used my research tools (notebook, camera, video camera, recorder). I believe that the need to record and archive each thing wasn't just tied to a scientifically oriented anxiety. I probably used those technological devices to hide my body, to reduce excessive display, to put myself on the margins in a context in which I didn't feel at ease. Perhaps it was a way to continue to maintain a certain "control" over my body, a body that began to give out a series of signals that were previously unknown to me. Work in the field, research, was a way of entering into a context that had been foreign to me up to that point, and it was a way to incorporate an element that had previously remained outside my work: my body.

My disciplinary reference point isn't art, nor sociology, nor anthropology. I am a professor of geography. In geography the body has been an object of study at least since the beginning of the 90s. While it still remains a "niche" subject, its legitimacy is not questioned in institutional research. But only if your own body is not in the picture. Despite the fact that we have begun to speak about emotions in geographical research, one's own emotions are still not welcome in mainstream institutional geography, neither in France nor in Italy. The same thing is true for sexuality.

Bringing these perspectives back to scientific study, despite the legitimacy of the self-ethnographic method in the social sciences (still very little in geography), delving deep, integrating your body, your sensations, your emotions, your sexuality, your positionality into the writing and the images, is still a complex operation that comes with a certain level of risk.

The risk is always in relation to one's position and the privilege that one enjoys. Being aware of one's privilege means knowing where one comes from, knowing where one *is* in the moment the action occurs, knowing the space in which one can act. This means willingly deciding the level of risk to run, understanding one's limits, overcoming the inevitable fear. How do you not let fear take over? To not succumb to fear of running risks you need to find places and people you let yourself be contaminated by, people with which to empower yourself through the transmission of knowledge and the creation of relationships. The workshops, in this sense, are a space of movement and of essential relations, an "espace bienveillant,"[8] wherein the individual body is transformed into the collective body: 'The workshops, for me, are the most radical, the most profound and most political experience that I learned to actualize, to name and to valorize through the postpornographic practice."[9]

The energy and the courage continue to circulate outside the workshop as well, potentially going on to contaminate all those spaces the participants' bodies traverse in their daily lives. Your body is no longer alone. It is a body that conveys relationships and creates spaces. The field shows me that my naked body is powerful. I feel my body in the field. The bodies of the subjects of my research take shape. The relationship of my body with theirs creates my field, it transforms my body. And I find a path for exploring ways of queering scientific research, of freeing it from the injunction of the printed page. Of giving it (my) body.

Flashback, International House for Women,[10] closing night of the series of encounters called Queer it Yourself, Kespazio!, Rome, May 18th, 2012. Guest: Slavina with her reading King Kong Ladies. Queer it Yourself was initiated by a queer and postcolonial research group with the aim of retelling some aspects of queer theory in a way that was less academic-elitist. Slavinia is one of the first postporno activists, writers, performers, sex educators. In those days, my research on postporno was underway. Slavina and Diana Pornoterrorista were my main sub/objects of study. I was, therefore, tasked with introducing Slavina's piece and escorting her during the seminar. Slavina's contribution was to end with a performance in the House's courtyard, a reading of feminist authors. I realized that in the preceding days I felt an unusual euphoric desire to share that moment with her. Not her lecture, the performance. What kind of legitimacy did I have to feel such a desire? Could I ask my subject to share, actively-perform her space? I had just read a text that moved me. I write: "Dear

---

8   Cha Prieu, "Thinking about Queer Places: Between Domination, Violence and Benevolence: Study in the Light of Parisian and Montreal Circles," Doctoral thesis (Paris: University of Paris-Sorbonne, 2015).

9   Slavina, interview by author, at *Looking for the Woman* workshop, (Sorbonne, 2016).

10   The International House for Women (Casa internazionale delle donne) in Rome has been an important center for the Italian women's movement since the early 1980s. https://www.casainternazionaledelledonne.org/.

Slavina, can I also read some texts with you?" She responds: "Dear Rachele, obviously." For me, it wasn't at all obvious to think of producing a text on a stage instead of a page. Neither was there anything obvious about the fact that the subjects of study would share space with the researcher.

I prepare the text, I practice the reading. The seminar begins. The moment of getting on stage is still far off. "What will we wear?" I ask; "Let's see, we have time, that's not important now," she responds. That moment of debriefing never comes. The moment for the stage arrives too soon. We are both standing behind the curtain. In a few minutes the performance will start. Slavina looks at me with complicity, with a radiant and reassuring smile on her face she says: "Listen, what do you say if we go up there naked?" I look at her. "Don't worry about the cold, we will have open jackets and shoes so our feet don't get cold." She climbs the stairs, passes by me, and I follow her. Music, reading. Music, reading. I read the words that come out of my mouth, they pass through my body and circulate in the air. I discover that the nudity is empowering, that my body is strong. I understand what it means to choose one's own field, to be in an open space, to contaminate your practices and your spaces.

FIGURE 8.1   King Kong Ladies performance, May 18th, 2012
PHOTO COURTESY OF RACHELE BORGHI

4   Chapter 2. Interstitial Spaces

Performance doesn't have to limit itself to representing just the object of study; instead, it can contribute to showing the normative and heteronormative nature of university institutions and disciplines, geography in primis.[11] Since 2011, pornoactivist performances have become central to my research on the relationship between spaces/bodies/norms. Slavina talks about pornoactivism to speak to performative actions that use the naked body as support for the action and that make dissident, declared, and vindicated sexualities visible. The bodies of pornoactivists are sexed, desiring political bodies that insert sexuality into militancy. If the revolution of the bedroom has been done, it is now time to bring the bedroom into the revolution. Sexuality is rarely explicit in militancy. Pornoactivism makes it explicit, and uses it.

Is it possible for pornoactivism to also enter the university as a legitimate practice and research method?

In 2008 Sam/Marie-Hélène Bourcier organized the seminar "Fuck My Brain" at the School for Advanced Studies in Social Sciences.[12] The reference to a sexual practice in the title of the seminar, gave a performative slant to a scientific event in an institutional context. The political worth of such a title, and the subject matter of the seminar, allow us to imagine that it is possible to open spaces to reflection/creativity that integrate dissident sexualities not only in content (the object of study), but also in practice (the title of the event) inside the institutional space: pornoactivism bursts into the university. Pornoacademism, or rather, pornoactivism done by academics inside the academy, allows sexuality from an intersectional perspective to be seen, it allows it to be inserted into the process of knowledge production that is considered legitimate, and it allows the body to reclaim its space.

This is the lens from which Zarra Bonheur was born.

Zarra Bonheur translates scientific study into performance with the aim of going beyond the limits that separate contexts (scientific/militant), knowledge (high culture/low culture, legitimate scientific knowledge/militant knowledge), spaces (university classroom/social center/theatrical scene), forms (conference/performance); going on to create interstitial spaces of subversion/transgression of the norms. In "Porno Trash" and "Degen(d)ereted Euphoria," my scientific research on the relationship between bodies and spaces, and

---

11   David Bell and Gill Valentine, *Mapping Desire: Geographies of Sexualities* (London: Routledge, 1995).

12   The School for Advanced Studies in Social Sciences (École des hautes etudes en sciences sociales), is a prestigious, elite graduate school in Paris.

FIGURE 8.2   Zarra Bonheur collective, underwear photo
PHOTO COURTESY OF RACHELE BORGHI

on the representation/perception of nudity in public spaces is transformed
into performances in which scientific knowledge becomes embodied. Zarra
Bonheur gives (the) body to research, brings the body where it is not expected,
frees these ideas from the pages of scientific magazines, rejects authority, and
contaminates spaces.

5   Chapter 3. From the Individual Body to the Collective Body

Zarra Bonhuer is neither a person nor an alter ego. Today, Zarra Bonheur is a
collective project of dissidence, resistance, experimentation and pornoactiv-
ism/pornoacademism. Zarra Bonheur is also an alliance experiment between
researcher (myself) and research subject (Slavina).

Zarra Bonheur is a transnational collective project of variable geometry
research and performance on gender, public space, and dissident sexualities.

[...] the project joins art and activism, inserting its actions in local contexts, involving collectives and individuals, making fixed and ephemeral
collaborations.

Zarra loves the workshop format as a form of participatory art. Sharing the
scene as a form of programmatic empowerment, Zarra Bonheur has many
voices and many bodies. We are all Zarra Bonheur.

We created a platform of exchange, contamination and creation, starting with various support systems, from conferences to performances via various forms of workshops and performative conferences. Zarra Bonheur is a spurious exercise in the contamination of places and people, of the transmission of competences, of self-education, a horizontal space that attempts to "socialize knowledge without establishing powers."[13]

Zarra Bonheur's work takes place in various contexts (militant, associative, institutional). It is, in this sense, an experiment in the translation of scientific research in order to make it more accessible, strip it of its elitist nature, and free texts from the prisons of scientific magazines. At the same time, it is the translation of militant knowledge and practices and the people's education in institutional instruction.

Teaching experiments born from the alliance between researcher (myself) and subject of research (Slavina) have always had the consent of the student-people. Despite this, each pedagogical initiative was accompanied by a "camouflage" job when it came to terms and titles, to allow it to "pass."

Flashback. In 2015, I proposed organizing an atelier along with Slavina as part of the March 8th women's day events at the university. The work was meant to draw attention to gender stereotypes and their internalization from an intersectional perspective through participatory practices. The title of the workshop contained the word "feminism." The university's culture committee forced me to remove the word "feminism" because it was considered exclusionary. When I asked for the support of the members of the advisory board, who were part of the committee because they were deemed gender "experts," no one answered me. Later when I asked for an explanation for their silence, I was told: "We had no intention of organizing a militant event."

#So-I-ask-myself: is it possible to incorporate content, modalities, and approaches without having the teaching get discredited?

If it's true that getting a good answer is dependent on asking a good question, maybe the question is: is it possible to definitively abandon the need to feel legitimized, accepted, and "in one's place" when you stray from the institution's paths?

When different practices are solitary, when dominant discourses are deep-rooted, the difficulty of overcoming resistance increases. If resistance and lack of faith are produced both by others and by oneself, maybe changing point of view isn't enough. We must change the direction toward which we turn our gaze.

---

13   This quote is frequently attributed to Primo Moroni, a Milanese writer and activist.

FIGURE 8.3   Cherchez la femme laboratory, Sorbonne, March 8th, 2016
PHOTO COURTESY OF RACHELE BORGHI

Despite the fact that micropolitics are not enough to change the world, it is more and more important to circulate examples, knowledges, practices, and energies, to intensify relationships and affections, and to create alliances that help us find the courage for parrhesia.[14]

Turning our gaze toward the margin instead of the center allows us not only to see the margins, but above all to see that they are inhabited, that for every center-space there is a corresponding occupied margin, freed spaces that can become the ground on which to build utopia.

---

14   Foucault, 1984.

Works Cited

Bell, David and Gill Valentine. *Mapping Desire: Geographies of Sexualities*. London: Routledge, 1995.

Borghi, Rachele, Lucía Egaña Rojas and Slavina. *Polyphonies sur la postpornographie.* "Mirroir/mirroirs," n. 5, 2015, p. 93–108.

Borghi, Rachele, Sam/Marie-Hélène Bourcier and Cha Prieur. "Performing Academy: Feedback and Diffusion Strategies for Queer Researchers." In The Routledge Research Companion to Geographies of Sex and Sexualities. Edited by Gavin Brown and Kath Browne. London: Routledge, 2016.

Bourcier, Sam/Marie-Hélène. *Homo.inc.* Paris: Cambourakis, 2017.

"Casa Internazionale Delle Donne." April 24, 2021. Accessed April 25, 2021. https://www.casainternazionaledelledonne.org/.

Cresswell, Tim. *In Place/Out of Place. Geography, Ideology, and Transgression.* Minneapolis: University of Minnesota Press, 1996.

Foucault, Michel. "Other Spaces." In Architecture, Movement, Continuity 1, no. 5 (1984):46–49.

hooks, bell. *Yearnings: Race, Gender and Cultural Politics*. Boston: South and Press, 1989.

King Kong Ladies. Performed by Slavina and Rachele. Rome: International House for Women, 2012.

Lorde, Audre. *Sister Outsider*. New York: Crossing Press, 1984.

Prieur, Cha. "Thinking about Queer Places: Between Domination, Violence and Benevolence: Study in the Light of Parisian and Montreal Circles." Doctoral thesis. Paris: University of Paris-Sorbonne, 2015.

Prieur, Cha. *The Courage of Truth*. Paris: Gallimard/Le Seuil, 2009.

CHAPTER 9

Transcyborgdyke

A Transfeminist and Queer Perspective on Hacking the Archive

Diego Marchante "Genderhacker"

A [trans]lesbian body can be defined as an organic cyborg, as a dangerous monster produced through fusions and confusions in the evolution of various species; but a [trans]lesbian body can also be considered an amalgam of techno-human fiber and material that possesses a "positive awareness" (a short-term memory, some might say, or, selective memory, others might say. Perhaps programmed?) about which no one can say a word, and not for any particular reason, but because there are very few gazes that are truly capable of capturing the body in question. If something has barely been named, this in itself does not mean it is a simulacrum, but rather it is the apparent symptom of trans-temporal and trans-spatial experiences, which, naturally, have never belonged to history. In this sense the [trans]lesbian body is trans-historic, it is a ghost that watches over those sleeping beauties at midnight, it is the shadow that disturbs the peaceful step of a citizen standing on a winter's night.[1]

$$\vdots$$

"Transcyborgdyke. A Transfeminist and Queer Perspective on Hacking the Archive" is a research project that began in 2006, at a time of political and artistic unrest, when Barcelona became a stage for a multitude of feminist, postporno and trans collectives to lay claim to greater visibility and sexual freedom through a multitude of gender dissidence and sexual guerilla practices. Interpellated by the political-artistic strategies of some of these collectives, we

---

1 Genderhacker Diego Marchante, "Transbutch. Border Struggles of Gender Between Art and Politics," Doctoral thesis in Advanced Studies in Artistic Investigation (Barcelona: University of Barcelona, 2016). (*Translation ours*).

began to contribute to the creation of some postporno performances done by the Post-Op collective and by Diana Pornoterrorista; later we became involved in organizing some of the first protests fighting against the pathologization of trans people. Our political practice as transgender and transfeminist militants woke our curiosity and our sense of responsibility and led us to begin researching the history of masculine lesbians and trans men in the Spanish context, through their political practices and their artistic creations.

The project has three fundamental aims. First, to create, from a transfeminist queer perspective, an archive of social movements and artistic practices that deal with questions of gender in the Spanish context. Second, to subvert the logic of the archive by using instruments of deconstruction and queer methodologies. Third, to create a study of female masculinities within our context.

To make this creative program we created Archivio T,[2] an online counter-archive from which to develop a historic frame made from the collection of Spanish political-artistic movements of the last forty years, and in which to merge three different stories rendered invisible by hegemonic history: the history of the feminist movement, the history of the lesbian movement, and the history of the trans movement.

In reality, this archive is a body, or rather, this archive is my body. This is the archive thanks to which I have grown as a person, as a militant, and as an artist. It is the history of all the references that have helped to (de)construct me as a transfeminist, lesbian, postporno, trans, adrift gender-pirate. This body-archive of mine did not appear from nothing, its existence would be impossible without the recognition of the genealogy of other gender and sexuality dissidents. Influenced by the political experience within the collectives, and by the contributions of queer theory, we began to ask ourselves how to transfer the activist practice into the structure of the archive. Could we subvert the ontological instruments of official knowledge when dealing with knowledge that destabilizes binary approaches to gender? How can we corrupt the archive using deconstructivist instruments like parody and transvestitism?

1   Queer Methodologies

A methodology is always fiction. Like a biography, a body, an identity [...] I propose, and I know I seem arrogant, intimacy as the future of research.[3]

---

2   The Archivio T cite can be found here: http://archivo-t.net.
3   Lucía Egaña, *Subnormal Methodologies*, Gramsci Seminar. (Barcelona: La cappella, 2012), 1. (*Translation ours*).

FIGURE 9.1   Transcyborgdyke poster, 2017

The project's methodology is based on the research method Jack Halberstam defined "queer methodology."[4] Thanks to this methodology, we have tried to weave together historical studies, sociological analysis, transfeminist and queer theoretical references and practices, archival research, taxonomical creations, audiovisual analysis, ethnography, case studies and participant observation, with the intention of exploring the close relationship between political and artistic practices that developed in Spanish queer and transfeminist movements. We started from our transgender and transfeminist activist experience, with the desire to call into question the principles of neutrality and objectivity inherent in knowledge production.[5]

We tried to transform our perspective using "the transgender look,"[6] "'queer looks,' 'oppositional gazes,' 'black looks,' and other modes of seeing not captured by the abbreviated structures of the male and female gaze."[7] Thanks to this transitory, transnational, transgender way of seeing we can expand our

---

4   Jack Halberstam, *Female Masculinity* (Durham: Duke University Press, 1998).
5   Donna Haraway, "Situated Knowledges," *Feminist Studies* v.14:3, 1998.
6   Jack Halberstam, *In a Queer Time and Place* (New York: NYU Press, 2005).
7   Ibid., 83.

fixed gaze on a time period from many points of view and,[8] from this inter-sectional perspective, we can take into account "gender as a dynamic category interconnected with other inequalities."[9]

Haraway, Halberstam, Platero and Egaña's experiences invite us to rethink the methodologies we adopt in our research projects from a feminist and queer perspective, inside or outside the academic environment, suggesting new paths to take in approaching the research processes with which to broaden our context, leave our cages, claim our personal experience as an object of study, and free ourselves from the pressures of coherence and impartiality.

2   Counter-Historical Archive

L. inherited a loss, a lost tradition. It's necessary to remember, inventing, to make memory by imagining, to unearth with each new word the names of those like L. It is in this moment that you learn to read in the language of the city, the hidden signs of a secret tradition: Archidyke [...] Follow the traces carefully: behind every space that is dominated by the network of discipline there is a point of escape from which the outside begins, a pathway of events.[10]

In "Counter-Historical Archives" we show six interconnected genealogies. To name them we parodically used slogans coined by the feminist movement to emphasize the militant nature of the research, to show the variety of feminist debates, and to represent the multiplicity of the feminist subject. In this phase of the research we articulated a few of the thematic threads developed in the last forty years by feminist, queer and trans movements, connecting a whole series of historic events, artists, collectives, shows, seminars, and artistic works that form the entirety of the relationships between Spanish art and politics.

In "Documents for All. From the Law on Social Danger to the Law on Gender Identity," we constructed a genealogy that goes from the Seventies to today through which we can observe the revolution started by the homosexual liber-ation movement, the women's liberation movement, and the transsexual lib-eration movement in Spain. A short journey from the first actions and street protests in the Seventies, when the francoist period had just ended and the

---

8   Ibid., 85.

9   Raquel (Lucas) Platero, "Is Intersectional Analysis a Feminist and Queer Methodology?" in *Other Forms of (re) Knowing, Reflections, Tools and Applications of Feminist Research* (Bilbao-Donostia: Vitoria-UPV/EHU, 2015), 79.

10   Paul Preciado, "We Say Revolution," In *Transfeminisms. Epistemes, Frictions and Flows*, edited by Miriam Solá and Elena Urko (Tafalla: Txalaparta, 2013).

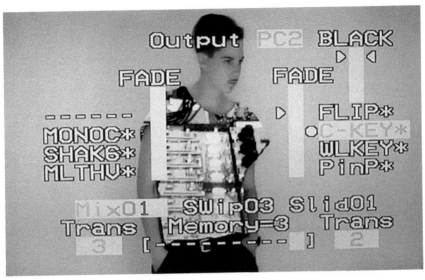

FIGURE 9.2   Image of the "genderhacking" laboratory, at SummerLAB, 2011

1970 law on social danger was in full force; passing from the rights, claims, and demonstrations of the 80s to obtain the law on divorce (1981) and abortion (1985)—a moment in which new alliances were formed, and varying disagreements between collectives arose—until we arrive at the beginning of the new century, with the approval of the law on same sex marriage (2005) and the law on equality and gender identity (2007). This journey shows us how people at the margins of society collectively organized against the oppressions they faced to claim access to citizenship and how, in this path full of alliances and discord, the first lines of escape toward other genealogies were born.

In "Ni porras, ni pistolas, tijeras para todas. On the Need for a Lesbian Imaginary,"[11] we laid out the first part of these escape routes that were started at the end of the 70s, when the first lesbians began to claim the specificity of their fight. They did it from within the homosexual movement, but many of them also fought within the feminist movement.[12] At the beginning of the 80s, with the very first lesbian celebration days, Spain saw the birth of the first

11   In this case we decided not to translate, so as not to lose the play on words between scissors as a weapon and as a metonym of lesbianism. The English translation is "No clubs, no pistols, scissors for all."

12   Gracia Trujillo, *Desire and Resistance. Thirty Years of Lesbian Mobilization in the Spanish State,* (Madrid: Egales, 2008).

FIGURE 9.3 Papers for all

collectives and alliances all across the country. Worried by their invisibility, they chose magazines and fanzines as their mode of expression.

With the appearance of "pink capitalism" in the 90s, some lesbian collectives and artistic groups were born who, influenced by queer theory, emphasized the need to create a lesbian culture.

In "The Axis of Evil is Heterosexual. The Eruption of the 'Queer Multitudes,'" we depicted the moment in which a group of collectives influenced by Anglo-Saxon queer theories began to mobilize within the Spanish context.

In the 90s, as the LGBT movement became more moderate, the queer Spanish movement found itself at the margins,[13] defending its autonomy and refusing any involvement in formal politics.[14] The term 'queer,' whose meaning refers to something strange, unique, deviant, became a word with great mobilizing power, a term that contained any kind of sexual difference, and permitted a challenge to the fixity of identity categories. When the first cases of AIDS came to light in Spain, many collectives reacted to the passiveness of the health institution and the LGBT movement. Radical Gai, Lsd (a lesbian group with

13   Gracia Trujillo, "Incomplete Files. An Analysis of the Absence of Representations of Feminine Masculinity in the Spanish Context (1979–1995)," in *Masculinities in Transition,* edited by Rafael M. Mérida and Jorge Luis Peralta (Madrid: Egales, 2015), 39–60.

14   Miriam Solá and Elena Urko Perez, *Transfeminisms. Epistemes, Frictions and Flows.* (Tafalla: Txalaparta, 2013).

FIGURE 9.4   The axis of evil is heterosexual

various names, among which Lesbians Without Money [*Lesbianas Sin Dinero*])
and Rqtr (Pink, I Love you Pink [*Rosa que te quiero rosa*]), along with other
international collectives, organized the first protests and the first AIDS preven-
tion campaigns. These first queer groups chose fanzines, posters, and flyers as
their modes of expression, developing hyper-identity and post-identity strategies of representation to replace identities and political strategies.

In "What's my gender? Whatever I want. Queer Theory and the Spanish
Artistic Context," we explored the moment in which, at the end of the 90s, new
feminist practices and queer theories entered into the institutional art space
along with the first generation of Spanish artists with a clear feminist awareness. The development of these practices that bordered politics and art was
possible thanks to the will of a group of artists and curators who, influenced
by feminist thought and emerging queer theories, were given space for their
debates on the denaturalization of sex and the performance of gender, and
over the course of three decades held a large number of shows, conferences
and seminars in institutions like Arteleku, Montehermoso, Koldo Mitexelena,
EACC, MACBA, MNCARS, Unia arteypensamiento, among others.

In "My Body, My Life, My Way of Fucking, Don't Kneel Before the Patriarchal
System. From Postporno to Pornopunkfeminist Activism," we articulated
a genealogy that allows us to observe the influence of debates on pornography between U.S. anti-sex and pro-sex feminism in the 80s and 90s. Pro-sex
feminism spread in Spain between the end of the 90s and the beginning of

FIGURE 9.5 My body, my life, my way of fucking, don't kneel before the patriarchal system

the following decade, when there was a boom in institutional and self-run encounters,[15] from which various "postporno" feminist collectives and, later "pornopunkfeminist" ones were born;[16] they began to politically claim public space through practices of sexual dissidence, and to claim a pornography produced with do-it-yourself methodologies.

Finally, with "Here, Is, the Trans Resistance. Transfeminisms and Trans Depathologization," we took a journey among the first claims of the transsexual movement in the 70s, passing from the birth of the first collectives of the trans movement in 2007 who were in favor of depathologization, up until the arrival of so-called transfeminism. The first mtf transsexual associations were born from within the homosexual movement and, after the first internal disagreements, they began to organize autonomously. The debate on transexuality entered into the feminist agenda in the early 90s. Shortly thereafter the first transsexual ftm associations were born. A decade later the trans movement began declaring itself in favor of depathologization with the aim of removing transsexuality, defined as a mental illness, from international psychiatric diagnostic manuals.

---

15   Solá and Urko Pérez, 2013.
16   Preciado, 2013.

FIGURE 9.6 What is my gender? Whatever I want

The feminist days that took place in Granada in 2009, open for the first time to ftm trans people, probably paved the way for so-called "transfeminism," a new alliance open to minority discourses that highlights the multiplicity of the feminist subject.[17]

The evolution of a whole series of theories that have taken on gender from a feminist perspective, and the development, starting in the 90s, of identity micropolitic, resulted in a political and aesthetic change visible in the artistic representation of the body, establishing new ties between theory, political practice and artistic representation.

Transcyborghery is a transfeminist and queer political-artistic archive. An artistic project that puts into conversation the content of the research, the ontological tools of the archive, and the bodies that spread these technological practices across the land. An experimental laboratory in which to begin to bend the ontological tools of official knowledge in the service of knowledges that destabilize the binary approach to gender, and with which to hack the archive with deconstructive tools like parody and transvestitism.

---

17   Miriam, Solá, "The Re-Politicization of Feminism, Activism and Identity Microdiscourses," in *Disagreements 7*, 264–81. Arteleku-Diputación Foral de Gipuzkoa—Centro José Guerrero-Diputación de Granada—Museu d'Art Contemporani de Barcelona (MACBA)—Museo Nacional Centro de Arte Reina Sofía (MNCARS)—UNIA arteypensamiento, (Donostia-Granada-Barcelona-Madrid-Sevilla, 2012).

Works Cited

Egaña, Lucía. *Subnormal Methodologies*. Gramsci Seminar. Barcelona: La cappella, 2012 http://www.bibliotecafragmentada.org/wp-content/uploads/2012/12/EGANA_Luc ia_Metodologias-Subnormales.pdf.

Genderhacker Diego Marchante. "Transbutch. Border Struggles of Gender Between Art and Politics." Doctoral thesis in Advanced Studies in Artistic Investigation. Barcelona: University of Barcelona, 2016. http://hdl.handle.net/2445/97243.

Halberstam, Jack. *In A Queer Time & Place*. New York: New York University Press, 2005.

Halberstam, Jack. *Female Masculinity*. Durham: Duke University Press, 1998.

Haraway, Donna. "Situated Knowledges: The Science Question in Feminism and the Privilege of Partial Perspective." *Feminist Studies* 14, no. 3 (1988): 575–99. doi:10.2307/3178066.

Platero, Raquel (Lucas). "Is Intersectional Analysis a Feminist and Queer Methodology?" In *Other Forms of (re) Knowing, Reflections, Tools and Applications of Feminist Research*. Bilbao-Donostia: Vitoria-UPV/EHU, 2015. http://publicaciones.hegoa.chu .es/assets/pdfs/329/Otras_formas_de_reconocer.pdf?1429005444.

Preciado, Paul B. "We say revolution." In *Transfeminisms. Epistemes, Frictions and Flows*. Edited by Miriam Solá and Elena Urko. Tafalla: Txalaparta, 2013.

Solá, Miriam. "The Re-Politicization of Feminism, Activism and Identity Micro-discourses." In *Disagreements* 7, 264–81. Arteleku-Diputación Foral de Gipuzkoa— Centro José Guerrero-Diputación de Granada—Museu d'Art Contemporani de Barcelona (MACBA)—Museo Nacional Centro de Arte Reina Sofía (MNCARS)— UNIA arteypensamiento, Donostia-Granada-Barcelona-Madrid-Sevilla, 2012. www .macba.cat/uploads/publicaciones/desacuerdos/textos/desacuerdos_7/Miriam _Sola.pdf.

Solá, Miriam and Elena Urko. *Transfeminisms. Epistemes, Frictions and Flows*. Tafalla: Txalaparta, 2013. www.gureliburuak.eus/documentos/primercapitulopdf/7865.pdf.

Trujillo, Gracia. *Desire and Resistance. Thirty Years of Lesbian Mobilization in the Spanish State*. Madrid: Egales, 2008.

Trujillo, Gracia. "Incomplete Files. An Analysis of the Absence of Representations of Feminine Masculinity in the Spanish Context (1979–1995)." In *Masculinities in Transition*, 39–60. Edited by Rafael M. Mérida and Jorge Luis Peralta. Madrid: Egales, 2015.

CHAPTER 10

Surveillance, Subjectivity and Public Space

A Gendered Look at Technologies

Carlotta Cossutta and Arianna Mainardi

In the last decades, security paradigms have been imposed that posit control as the principal response to social problems. Technologies are often strong allies, both because of their pervasiveness and because they are easier to take on than complex police apparatuses. This is further complicated by technology's relationship to a form of capitalism that turns surveillance into a source of profit (data commerce) and a way of analyzing and promoting constantly emerging needs.

We would like to explore the relationship between these widespread modes of control and the construction of gender identity, while continuing to pay attention to resistance above discipline. How is it possible to practice creative strategies for subverting the effects of control and the normalizing impulses produced by the pervasiveness of digital technologies? Let's try to reflect on this question, beginning with concepts of identity, public space and surveillance; concepts that can guide us in our critical analysis of the different forms of surveillance and their development.

By identity we do not mean something acquired and immutable, nor a solipsistic process that depends only on each of us. I do not construct my own identity by myself, but in a continuous exchange that occurs through recognition with the other: identity is a process based on relating and interrelationality. For this reason, we find particular relevance in the critical study of gender that sees gender (and the relations of power that come from it, like sexual binarism) as a social construct; our gender identities would be, therefore, the result of a performance, a series of acts we learn and reproduce constantly: a staging.[1] Identity is also the temporary result of relations we weave together, a daily performance, that can vary, and find new roads and new gestures.

As Hannah Arendt shows us, one of the principal places that makes identity visible and intelligible is public space, where public space is understood as the space in which identity emerges in relation to the other, allowing action

---

1   See Judith Butler, *Gender Trouble*, (New York: Routledge, 1990).

to occur. Arendt understands public space as a table that allows us to connect to one another and keeps us divided at the same time; "a world of things is between those who have it in common, as a table is located between those who sit around it;" this table is the public sphere that "relates and separates men at the same time."[2] In this public space action can be free to emerge in a creative way too, introducing new elements into the world thanks to the connections and the distance we put between each other. For Arendt, therefore, identity always needs the gaze of the other in order to emerge, through a process that gives rise to impromptu and unexpected results.

The gendered gaze is particularly relevant to this discussion because it allows us to see some of the ways power characterizes public space; for example, the dividing line between public and private that constitutes the battlefield of feminism in so far as it is a tool of exclusion/inclusion in public life. Feminism teaches us to ask ourselves: what of the identity of those who are historically and materially excluded from public space? In what forms and in what ways do these identities subvert the public sphere even as they make themselves visible? To answer these questions, we asked ourselves how much both identity and public space can be an object of forms of surveillance that operate like tools of control and simultaneously act like processes of subjectification.

The concept of surveillance has a broad, layered meaning, with a very long history, but in these pages we will primarily consider the modes of video control, in the forms of traceability made possible through the dissemination of digital technologies, in the relationship between visibility and invisibility in the online spaces of social networking sites. Reflecting on the idea of surveillance both as an exercise in security—here security is understood both as safety and as control—and as normalizer. Gender studies have thoroughly investigated these two aspects that constitute surveillance, interrogating the ways in which it influences the processes of subjectification and the possibilities for subjectivities that deviate from the heteropatriarchal norm—white, male, cis-heterosexual—to participate in the public space.

CCTV (closed circuit television) is an example of constant and pervasive surveillance that signals an important passage toward the automation of the processes of control. At the same time, or maybe precisely for this reason, CCTV is a notable example for understanding how these technologies of surveillance have been challenged and tested through political and artistic performances. These performances do not take shape via destruction or obfuscation, but rather through a creative process that reclaims control over these technologies

---

2 Hannah Arendt, *The Human Condition*, (Chicago: University of Chicago Press, 1958), 52.

FIGURE 10.1   Macho-free zone campaign poster

and where the work of critique is always accompanied by a process of participation and invention.

We refer here to the work of the Surveillance Camera Players (SCP), in particular to "1984," as an example of a performance that is explicit in its artistic and

political nature.[3] The Surveillance Camera Players emerge in 1996 in New York and are devoted to defending the right to privacy of every individual, the right to anonymity, and to not being spied on continuously in spite of ourselves. To this end they organize performance-protests in front of the surveillance cameras in public spaces, and they use their visibility, their public appearances, their interviews and their website to upend the common notion that "the only people opposed to surveillance are those with something to hide."[4] The Surveillance Camera Players prepared an outline-guide on their website for anyone who wants to embark on their path, showing step-by-step how to create a performance. First, you have to find where exactly the surveillance cameras are placed: archives of local papers may have useful announcements about the installation of closed-circuit cameras. There are different types of surveillance cameras, used in different places for different purposes; the ones the SCP consider are either in public places and are used by the police and other public authorities, or by private authorities. In any case, the performances are also recorded by at least one member of the group so as to have documentation if need be. Once the exact location of the camera, in front of which the performance will be carried out, is identified, this information must be indicated on flyers that will be distributed during the event.

The adaptation of George Orwell's *1984*, produced many times between November 1998 and April 1999, by six members of the group, is without a doubt among their more significant events. One of the more interesting aspects of this performance is, above all, the connection between Orwell's book and the politics of the Surveillance Camera Players; both point a finger at technology as a means of social control and mass-media instrumentalization. One of the recurring phrases in the group's work is, precisely: "Big brother is watching."

In a very strategic way, the Surveillance Camera Players turn their attention to the apparatuses of public video surveillance. They do this to increase awareness of the presence of surveillance cameras in the public sphere. In this way the artistic/political collective also creates new models of interaction, vision and discourse with, and through the technohuman surveillance interface, forcing an unexpected use of control of the camera; we see something similar in the theater. Since the Surveillance Camera Players perform in front of video surveillance cameras in the streets/ public squares/ subways, anyone that passes or crosses public space attends the same performance one can see

---

3   Surveillance Camera Players, "1984," https://youtu.be/RILTl8mxEnE.
4   The Surveillance Camera Players https://noemalab.eu/org/sections/specials/tetcm/teatro_te cno/scp/premessa.html.

FIGURE 10.2 Surveillance camera players, "we are the dead"

in the video recording, creating a link between the controlled and the controller that, for a few minutes, see the same scene represented just for them. Additionally, the Surveillance Camera Players often look directly at the camera, further reinforcing the relationship with the person who is supposedly watching the recordings.

This performance shows that it is possible to subvert both the results and the definitive order of CCTV, and it brings us back to the question of aperture: what possible ways are there of enacting creative strategies for subverting the effects of control and standardization produced by the pervasiveness of digital technologies?

Some of the digital environments in which we have been immersed are not made as something external with which we engage, but as different objects and tools of control that are increasingly naturalized in our daily lives. Additionally, we can no longer recognize or intercept the gaze of those observing us in the ways we could when the observer was behind the surveillance camera. Recognizing the institutions and discourses towards which the performances should be directed becomes, therefore, more complicated.

Kember and Zylinska suggest looking at contemporary technosocial relations to think about how life, in its entirety, has entered a process of constant mediation.[5] If, therefore, the new monitoring technologies can monitor every aspect of my identity, or rather, of my life, the practices that can be enacted must necessarily involve every aspect of my existence. The mediation offered by digital technologies can be read through technological, sociological and biological processes, processes that can still be subverted and interrogated through the concept of performance. It is no longer enough to act in front of the camera. The strategies of subversion must impact the construction of my identity, both online and offline. Here, the idea of gender is tied to the concept of performance because gender calls into question part of my relationship to the world.

According to Foucault, if we begin with these considerations, we can revisit the study of forms of subversion: "Doing so means overturning the traditional problem, no longer raising the questions 'How can a free subject penetrate the substance of things and give it meaning? How can it activate the rules of a language from within and thus give rise to the designs which are properly its own?' Instead, these questions will be raised: 'How, under what conditions and in what forms can something like a subject appear in the order of discourse?'"[6] This quotation can guide our thinking about the relationship between control and technology, and it helps us pay particular attention to the relationship between gender and new apparatuses born from merging digital technologies and neoliberal governmentality. The question that drives us, therefore, comes up once again and asks not about how a free subject can exist in these contexts, but about the possible emergence of a subject capable of practices of resistance within them. We begin from the typically Foucauldian awareness that there is no subject before or outside of the practices of power: none of us is *innocent* with regards to a power that contributes to reproducing and, at the same time, defining us as subjects. This reproductive cycle depends on the invisibility of the apparatuses of power and thus, a first step towards resistance can be giving life to and shining a light on the counter-actions.

Investigating questions like surveillance, identity and public space in the context of digital media, with the goal of imagining new creative spaces of subversion, allows us to look at the relationship between sexuality and the web. We choose to do this by observing the neoliberal context in which we find ourselves, and by using the category of visibility–a term very often linked to

---

5   Sarah Kember and Joanna Zylinska, *Life After New Media*, (Boston: MIT Press, 2012).
6   Michel Foucault, *Aesthetics, Method, Epistemology,* (New York: The New Press, 1998), 221.

social network sites, but that also permeates the biopolitical apparatuses that find their origins in pastoral power. In fact, through confession, pastoral power focuses on the individual's interiority, on their thoughts and emotions, forging a relationship that extends beyond the behavior-sanctioning by sovereign and juridical traditions, to an amplifying of the sense of productive, not just repressive surveillance. Confession has a strong productive power: it allows the narrating subject to know itself, giving the confessor the truth of their sins; likewise, the listener becomes the proprietor of this truth and contributes to its creation. This search for *truth* is precisely that productive moment in which the relation to power constructs the subject: through confession it becomes evident that there is a reversal of the sense of commonality, and interiority is nothing more than the exteriority of the confessional discourse. Confession is also the moment in which both the macrophysical and microphysical character of power emerges: it is, in fact, fruit of a societal-organizing directed toward single individuals and their interpersonal relationships.

One of the principal themes of confession is that of sexuality, understood not only as practiced acts, but also as the collection of desires, impulses and fantasies that involve the interiority of the subject. Sex, therefore, is the privileged object of confession, and as such it is not silenced, instead it becomes a powerful indicator of the *truth* of the subject, also thanks to its position between mind (desire and fantasies) and body (actions and practices). The link between power and sexuality, therefore, creates those deviances it claims to combat, making them explicit and using them as the fodder for its own discourse. Sexuality is, therefore, an apparatus and not an instinct that contrasts with culture; it is not a natural element that power represses, but a construct used to govern subjects. Therefore, confession and pastoral power invert the process of individualization and control, opening the way for the interrogation of liberal governmentality and biopolitics: in a feudal society, as is typical of sovereignty, the process of individualization is ascendant and primarily involves those with more power–those who will be more recognizable, more *individual*; in disciplinary societies, on the other hand, this process will be descendent, those with less power are more individualized, more visible.

This emphasis on visibility is accompanied by a redefinition of the distinction between public and private space, a distinction that is eroded by power and by subjects that want to make themselves visible. This internal visibility, however, does not open spaces of freedom or immediate subversion; instead, it fits perfectly with neoliberal governmentality and its protagonist: the *homo oeconomicus*. In fact, the break in the distinction between public and private anticipates many of the conversations about precarity and not just those in which each subject has to become an auto-entrepreneur, and be able to put a value on every aspect of their own lives, from their abilities to their relationships.

If control through a video camera, albeit pervasive, allowed for forms of resistance through the simple revealing of this surveillance, the complex weaving together of the desire to be included in public space, digital confessional practices, and surveillance and normalization outcomes have pushed us to ask ourselves how to obstruct this mechanism of control. We do not have one singular answer, obviously, but we believe that exposing the ties between modes of oppression, neoliberal governmentality, and mechanisms of (in)visibility can allow us to imagine different forms of resistance in and through digital environments; environments that are not only able to interrogate the relationship between the watcher and the watched (as with the Surveillance Camera Players), but are able to re-elaborate the construction of subjectivity itself within digital contexts. In this sense, the challenge could be to bring one's own embodied experience and situated knowledge to and through these digital environments in order to call into question the apparatuses: if confession requires sexuality, transfeminism can offer new tools to transform it into a politics of positionality that can subvert gender norms (but not only) which are reproduced within the relationship with digital technologies. Therefore, we must go back to the question we asked ourselves at the beginning, and look for traces of resistance, however minimal, within the individual (and collective) behaviors of whoever acts in and through digital technologies without imagining a resisting subject, but we must continue to keep our eyes peeled in order to identify its emergence, even if it should appear in new and collective forms.

Works Cited

Arendt, Hannah. *The Human Condition.* Chicago: University of Chicago Press, 1958.

Butler, Judith. *Gender Trouble: Feminism and the Subversion of Identity.* New York: Routledge, 1990.

Conrad, Kathryn. "Surveillance, Gender, and the Virtual Body in the Information Age." *Surveillance and Society* 6, no. 4 (2009):380–7.

Foucault, Michel. *Aesthetics, Method, and Epistemology.* New York: The New Press, 1998.

Kember, Sarah and Joanna Zylinska. *Life After New Media: Mediation as a Vital Process.* Boston: MIT Press, 2012.

Lyon, David. *Surveillance Society: Monitoring Everyday Life.* Buckingham: Open University Press, 2001.

The Surveillance Camera Players. *NOEMA*. Accessed April 25, 2021. https://noemalab
.eu/org/sections/specials/tetcm/teatro_tecno/scp/premessa.html.

The Surveillance Camera Players."1984," youtube video, Oct. 12th, 2006. https://st1
.zoom.us/web_client/yckmkh4/html/externalLinkPage.html?ref=https://www
.youtube.com/watch?v=RILTl8mxEnE.

Translators' Epilogue

Julia Heim and Sole Anatrone

Digital Fissures is a transnational transfeminist exploration into the ways that technologies, bodies, and identities interrelate, mutate, and co-habitate within and without contemporary western systems of power. Each chapter is a manifesto of sorts, elaborating the activist, artistic, and academic work of their authors; readers gain insight into the transfeminist creations these chapters describe, while also bearing witness to the activism that is in the writing itself of these chapters. In this way you, reader, are invited into the march.

For us, the translators, our marching, and our transfeminist activism has taken us to many different cities and neighborhoods, including the streets of Rome and Bologna where we began our collaboration with the editors of the original Italian version of this book, *Smagliature digitali: corpi, generi e tecnologie* (Agenzia X, 2018).

From rethinking feminist archives, to inserting postpornography in academia, to approaching sex toys from a transpositive perspective, to dismantling the foundations of technocapitalism, the areas of inquiry in *Digital Fissures* are lenses through which to explore the relationships between genders, bodies and technologies. All the various chapters engage with the work of activist-scholars like Paul Preciado and Donna Haraway, whose thinking lays the groundwork for reimagining the body as hybrid, as malleable and as a subversive source of potentiality. Building on these precursors, these essays offer us road maps for unimagined and uncharted social scapes. The text is animated by questions of artificial reproduction, surrogacy, digital advocacy, and the relationship between citizenship and technology. It investigates the ways technology changes the contours of pleasure, of the archive, of surveillance; and it explores the ways in which radical approaches to the cyber and the cyborg might transform and are transforming the ways we inhabit and think about identity-defining categories like gender and sexuality. The authors call for a critical approach to our current apparatuses of power and highlight the potential within technologies to disturb misogynist, transphobic, racist structures, and to reclaim the margins as spaces of radical potential. To use the words of the Italian editors, Carlotta Cossutta, Valentina Greco, Arianna Mainardi, and Stefania Voli, "Speaking of the relationship between bodies-technologies-genders means positioning oneself within the space of monstrosity and abjection." Through this embodied discomfort we are invited to question existing techno-social norms, and imagine transfeminist futures: What is the relationship between bodies and technologies? How do they shape one another? What are the ways that the apparatuses of power standardize bodies and technologies? How can we use our marginalized positions to challenge "naturalized" systems and create new digital and corporal pathways? How can we map the subversions that have come before and build upon them?

By presenting this translation we invite English speakers to take part in this international conversation. We are all the future of transfeminist activism. Join us in continuing this critical project.

Index

Milton Keynes UK
Ingram Content Group UK Ltd.
UKHW021423161123
432691UK00031B/701